Illinois Central College
Learning Resource Center

American Short
Speeches

Abraham Lincoln Speaking at Gettysburg. The frontispiece is a photograph of the painting by Fletcher G. Ransom. It is reproduced by special arrangement with the Commercial Photography Division, United Press International.

American Short Speeches

AN ANTHOLOGY

Selected and Edited by

Bower Aly
Department of Speech, The University of Oregon

Lucile Folse Aly
Department of English, The University of Oregon

THE MACMILLAN COMPANY, *New York*
COLLIER-MACMILLAN LIMITED, *London*

This book is dedicated to the spirit of Thucydides, of whom Cicero observed that "he almost equals the number of his words by the number of his thoughts."

Foreword

SPEECHES NEED NOT last forever to endure, as this collection demonstrates. Here are collected some of the most eloquent American speeches, from colonial to contemporary times, most lasting no more than five minutes, yet so appropriate to the occasions from which they arise that they reach deep roots of human response which give them significance in any time.

The occasions of these speeches are ones in which human values and human dignity are at stake, and the speakers are persons who perceive and express this conflict clearly. Their success comes from their eloquent human response to the choices, pressures, hopes, and fears of the reality that they face.

We often respond with action when facing great needs, and action presumably speaks for itself. But speech can speak for all men and illuminate what action wishes to say. When these selections are seen in this light they reflect the deeper meanings of human beings confronting themselves.

Dr. Lucile Aly is assistant professor of English and Dr. Bower Aly is professor of speech at the University of Oregon. Both distinguished scholars in their fields, they have placed each speech in its historical setting and have provided readers with carefully chosen references, which will allow further investigation of these short and significant American speeches.

Arthur C. Hastings
Stanford University

Preface

INASMUCH as this anthology is a late harvest from ideas planted over the years, the editors are indebted to their students and other friends who have contributed, sometimes unwittingly, to its fruition. Many of these friends cannot be named here, but the helpfulness of others who have made recent contributions to the book should be acknowledged. It is a pleasure for the editors, while absolving them of responsibility for the demerits of the book, to thank the following persons whose counsel concerning one or more chapters has been generous and helpful: J. M. Bain, Edwin R. Bingham, Stuart Gerry Brown, Marc Connelly, Carol Evans, Wilbur E. Gilman, Elizabeth Stevenson Ives, Alvin M. Josephy, Jr., Manuel Irwin Kuhr, Elizabeth Kunimoto, Kathryn Lewis, David E. Lilienthal, Frances Lea McCurdy, John G. Neihardt, Houston Peterson, Earl Pomeroy, Edward Rogge, Martin Schmitt, Adlai E. Stevenson III, Karl R. Wallace, and Hollis L. White.

The editors, also indebted to their secretaries and research assistants whose intelligence and insight were devoted to the manuscript, express their gratitude to Gladys Ide, Velma Francisco, Rhoda Lomsky, Mark Perry, and Carl and Gwen Clavadetscher.

Eugene, Oregon   B. A.
                                                                 L. F. A.

Contents

*American Short
Speeches*

Introduction

THIS ANTHOLOGY proceeds from some convictions, of which four may be stated: (1) that public speaking has been the characteristic art of the American people, (2) that much may be said in five minutes, (3) that speeches are significant transactions in the human commonwealth, and (4) that the art of speechmaking can be learned.

Anyone who endeavors to understand the American past must be impressed with the function of oratory in American life. Despite the inhibitions imposed by conformity, as noted by Alexis de Tocqueville, the Americans of the nineteenth century had as full an opportunity for public discussion of issues and as free a practice in the art of speechmaking as any society known to man. Exceptions, such as the unwillingness of Southerners at some periods prior to the Civil War to permit speechmaking concerning "the peculiar institution," merely proved the rule. The nineteenth century common man in the United States enjoyed a freedom to speak and to hear likely to be exercised even in free Britain only by a member of Parliament. In the frontier environment, speechmaking was an art open to anyone who had the time to speak or to listen. A trial for murder in a rural courthouse presented drama in which the leading actor might really be hanged after the curtain went down. The frontier preacher in the summer encampment exhorted the frontiersman to forsake his sinful ways *now*. The campaign speech, through which Federalist or Republican, Mugwump or Barnburner, sought the suffrage of his neighbors, brought the farmers from their fields to experience an excitement not known in all societies.

Doubtless many speeches were longer than they needed to be. Some may have been so long—and so tedious—as to defeat the speaker's purpose. To be sure, a speech was expected to convey something more than a verbal message. Its primary function was often simply to please or to entertain. Some commemorative speeches were well-nigh ritualistic. In the past, perhaps more consistently than today, Americans tended to consider a public undertaking not quite legitimate until sanctified by a speech. In the annals of the history of speechmaking in America one will find dedicatory speeches for canals long since filled, for railway trains apparently going the way of the river steamboat, and for buildings now fallen into ruin. One almost forgotten manifestation of the speaker's art in America is the "hanging" speech, a genre extinguished not only by the electric chair and the gas chamber but also by the squeamishness of modern Americans, who require expiation of guilt to be conducted in private and thus deprive the condemned man of an audience for any speech, long or short.

Public speaking was thus both a form of power, like wealth or generalship, and a form of art superficially akin to literature, music, and painting. In a relatively free society, the role of the orator, either in creating a public opinion prerequisite to action or in verbalizing the hopes and fears thought to exist in his constituency, had to be reckoned with; the man of the word, like the man of the dollar and the man of the sword, was a man of power. The relation between economic man and rhetorical man was reciprocal. The play of forces set in motion or manipulated by the orator determined—as well as was determined by —the directions taken by the banker and the soldier. An aeon of four years lies between John Brown speaking at Charlestown and Abraham Lincoln speaking at Gettysburg.

The function of oratory as a form of art was somewhat more subtle than its obvious function as a form of power. The essence of American oratory was found in its folk quality: it was (and remains) the art of the common man. All the other arts were at least one step removed from what the man on the tow-road or the canal construed as reality. To the extent that the orator strove for literary "effect" he was in danger of losing his immediate hearers, who were primarily interested in questions of the moment rather than in issues to be determined by posterity. Hence even the greatest speeches were sometimes ephemeral. Only on occasion, and more or less by chance, did a speech achieve that quality of universality sometimes supposed to be necessary to literature. But a speech is not a misbegotten essay; it is not a bastard poem. It has its own special laws, limitations, and possibilities derived from the principles of rhetoric and from the circumstance that the hearer is truly the end and object of the speech. Oratory is thus perforce a communicative art under a requirement not imposed fully on any other art.

Perhaps something should be said concerning the term "American" as employed in this anthology. Presumably the claims of Logan, Spotted Tail, and Chief Joseph to this title are not impaired; they were of the first Americans. Winston Churchill was made an honorary citizen of the United States by an Act of Congress. Harold Macmillan, like Winston Churchill, was born of an American mother, and Macmillan's speech was a tribute to an American president. If anyone objects to designating King Kalakaua an American, the editors must admit the technical objections and confess to having exercised editorial license to confer posthumous Americanism on Kalakaua. The exercise of editorial license they believe justified in view of the loyalty of the descendants of the subjects of Kalakaua. And if Kalakaua had lived a little longer he would doubtless have achieved American citizenship on his own, as did his cousin Prince Kuhio! The editors can conceive no objection to naming Douglas Mac-Arthur, Adlai Stevenson, David E. Lilienthal, John F. Kennedy, and the other speakers included, as Americans.

Considering the long experience of Americans with the delight, the excitement, and even sometimes the edification to be derived from speechmaking, one may well ponder the question: Why has not the short speech developed an art form of its own? The failure to develop the short speech as a genre subject to its own principles seems all the more remarkable when one considers that the most famous speech in American history— Lincoln's Gettysburg Address—took less than three minutes to deliver. It is noteworthy also that the short story has enjoyed a vogue in the United States, the short essay has prospered, and the short lyric poem has never lacked for devotees. The one-act play has long since come into its own.

Of course, some speeches must be long. Edward Everett wrote to Abraham Lincoln, after they shared the same platform at Gettysburg, "I should be glad if I could flatter myself that I came as near the central idea of the occasion in two hours as you did in two minutes." Lincoln, both courteous and correct, replied, "In our respective parts yesterday you could not have been excused to make a short address, nor I a long one." [1]

Not all of Lincoln's speeches were as short as his "few re-marks" at Gettysburg. The public speaker making a declaration of public policy may require an hour or more. An audience ex-pecting a long speech may be disappointed with a short one. Yet on reviewing the prolix utterances of public men in and out of Congress, one is inescapably led to the conclusion that sometimes their speeches are long not because they need be, but because (1) the speaker has never seriously studied the art and craft of speechmaking, or because (2) the speaker has not had, or at least has not taken, the time to do his homework, and hence must do it while, rather than before, he speaks. Like the talkative lady advised to avoid verbosity, the speaker does not know what he thinks until he has heard what he has said. Perhaps never before in the history of the human race have so many incompetent speakers delivered so many dull speeches to so many long-suffering audiences as in the United States since World War II.

This book is sent forth in the hope that it may demonstrate to those who read it that a speech need not be everlasting in order to be memorable, that noteworthy American speeches have not always been as long as Daniel Webster's magnificent reply to Senator Hayne, and that, in strict fact, a competent speaker, well-briefed, can say a great deal in five or ten minutes.

As a matter of fact, memorable speeches even shorter than any of the twenty provided in this volume have been known to celebrate an occasion, influence a jury, or affect public policy.

Henry Clay, pointing his long finger at a culprit under a de-fective indictment in a Kentucky court, shouted the two-word speech: "Go home!" The defendant, doubtless no more startled than the judges and the jury, fled, leaving to Clay the task of explaining his departure.[2]

When a shrewd delegate from South Carolina, on his way to attend the Continental Congress, visited the Virginia House of Burgesses to discover what was happening in the Old Dominion, he heard a short speech by Colonel George Washington and

[1] Paul Revere Frothingham, *Edward Everett: Orator and Statesman* (Boston: Houghton Mifflin Co., 1925), p. 458.

[2] Bernard Mayo, *Henry Clay: Spokesman of the New West* (Boston: Houghton Mifflin Co., 1937), p. 108.

thought it the most eloquent one delivered. It consisted of a single sentence: "I will raise one thousand men towards the relief of Boston, and subsist them at my own expense."[3]

William Pitt, responding to a toast that credited him with saving England, said with becoming modesty and rare eloquence:

> I return you many thanks for the honour you have done me; but Europe is not to be saved by any single man. England has saved herself by her exertions, and will, as I trust, save Europe by her example.[4]

When John F. Kennedy was campaigning against Henry Cabot Lodge for a seat in the United States Senate, the Kennedy family joined enthusiastically in his support. It was left for Robert Kennedy, called from campaign headquarters, to make one of the shortest political speeches on record:

> My brother Jack couldn't be here, my mother couldn't be here, my sister Eunice couldn't be here, my sister Pat couldn't be here, my sister Jean couldn't be here, but if my brother Jack were here, he'd tell you Lodge has a very bad voting record. Thank you.[5]

If proof were needed to support the assertion that speeches are important transactions in the human commonwealth, surely the speeches recorded in this anthology would provide it. In the pathetic speech of Logan mourning his murdered family, as in Macmillan's speech of tribute to the murdered president, one observes the struggles and the passions of mankind. One discovers speechmaking, whatever its limitations, to be the most human of the arts.

In the simple chronological progression of American speeches from 1774 to 1963, one may find Benjamin Franklin in his old age anticipating the prosperity of the new republic and hear Woodrow Wilson admonishing the young men at the Naval Academy. One may listen to Franklin Roosevelt's colloquial address to the Daughters of the American Revolution and hear David E. Lilienthal's confession of faith. Robert G. Ingersoll

---

[3] Sir Otto George Trevelyan, *The American Revolution* (London: Longmans, Green, and Co., 1909), Vol. I, p. 192.

[4] John Holland Rose, *William Pitt* (London: G. Bell and Sons, 1923), p. 538.

[5] James MacGregor Burns, *John Kennedy: A Political Profile* (New York: Harcourt, Brace & World, Inc., 1961), p. 114.

grieving at the funeral of his brother, David Kalakaua admonishing the people of Lahaina, William Faulkner expressing a
passionate hope for the future of mankind, Adlai E. Stevenson
saying words of farewell to Lloyd Lewis, Winston Churchill
offering his compatriots blood, toil, tears, and sweat, John F.
Kennedy declaring himself to be a citizen of Berlin—all are
engaged in the varied human transactions that characterize
speechmaking. Nicola Sacco protesting his innocence, George
Graham Vest eulogizing man's best friend; Douglas MacArthur
accepting the surrender of Japan, and John Brown denouncing
slavery—all exemplify the differing purposes served by the public speaker. Frederick Douglass, like Abraham Lincoln, finding
words to praise those who died in battle, performs an office as
old as that of Pericles and as new as Viet-Nam. Chief Joseph
and Chief Spotted Tail seem to be performing a like office for
a whole people.

In the selection of the texts to be included in this anthology,
the editors have endeavored to include only speeches actually
delivered to an audience, to employ a full text, unabridged, and
to state the source of the text. The initial aim, soon abandoned,
was to include no speech longer than Lincoln's address at Gettysburg. In other respects also the editors have modified their original intent. The speech by George Graham Vest is but the
peroration of a longer courtroom speech, but it is all that survives,
and it stands alone. The speeches by the Indian chieftains—
Logan, Spotted Tail, and Joseph—are open to question not only
as to translation but also as to provenience. But, while observing
scrupulously the obligation to state the source of the text they
have adopted, the editors have not chosen to delete a text simply because its accuracy may be open to question. To apply
that rule would perhaps be sound for speeches as history, but
dubious for speeches as literature. Who would discard the
speeches of Hamlet because they were conceived by William
Shakespeare rather than by the Prince of Denmark?

No discipline currently taught in American universities has
a more venerable tradition than public speaking. Ever since
Isocrates established speechmaking as the core curriculum for
the School from which "as from the Trojan horse, none but

heroes proceeded," [6] the art of speechmaking has been recognized as one worthy to be learned and susceptible to being taught. Ever since Quintilian formulated his system of instruction on the assumption that "the perfect orator cannot exist unless as a good man," [7] universities, when founded, have acknowledged a responsibility to teach the art of public speaking. The pedagogical battles have thus been not so much concerning *whether*, as how and *when*.

Chauncey A. Goodrich began his preface to *Select British Eloquence* with Mr. Hume's remark that "he who would teach eloquence must do it chiefly by *examples*." [8] Apparently the dictum of Hume—and of Goodrich—is accepted today; for courses in speechmaking generally provide, even if only for definition, examples of speeches. Some students, however, tend to be discouraged by the models provided. The long exemplary speeches, often those of statesmen who spoke under no cloture rule, further the impression—all too easy to reach—that nothing significant can be said in five minutes. Perhaps the twenty examples provided in *American Short Speeches* will serve to demonstrate to unbelievers that something handsome may happen to a speech when circumstances require its compression.

In any event, the editors of this anthology suggest that the idea of the short speech as a genre is worthy of consideration, if only for the practical purposes of the classroom; and they offer the idea, and this book, in the spirit of James Harris, who declared in his preface to *Hermes:*

The chief End, proposed by the Author of this Treatise in making it public, has been to excite his Readers to curiosity and inquiry; not to teach them himself by prolix and formal Lectures, (from the efficacy of which he has little expectation) but to induce them, if possible, to become Teachers to themselves, by an impartial use of their own understandings. He thinks nothing more absurd than the common notion of instruction, as if Science were to be poured into the Mind,

[6] Cicero, *On Oratory and Orators*, J. S. Watson (ed.), (London: George Bell and Sons, 1884), pp. 246–247.

[7] Quintilian, *Institutes of Oratory*, John Selby Watson (ed.), (London: George Bell and Sons, 1882), p. 4.

[8] Chauncey A. Goodrich, *Select British Eloquence*, with an introduction by Bower Aly (Indianapolis: Bobbs-Merrill Co., 1963), p. v.

like water into a cistern, that passively waits to receive all that comes. The growth of Knowledge he rather thinks to resemble the growth of Fruit; however external causes may in some degree co-operate, it is the internal vigour, and virtue of the tree, that must ripen the juices to their just maturity.[9]

---

[9] James Harris, Esq., *Hermes: or A Philosophical Inquiry Concerning Universal Grammar*, 4th ed., revised and corrected (Dublin: James Williams, 1773), p. v.

CHAPTER 1

Speech to Lord Dunmore

LOGAN

Who is there to mourn for Logan?—Not one.

—LOGAN

The Speaker

JAMES LOGAN, commonly known as "Logan" or "Chief Logan" was born about 1725 and died in 1780. It is supposed that he took his name as a tribute to James Logan, the botanist and colonial leader, who was secretary for some years to William Penn and, like Penn, a magnanimous and peace-loving friend to the Indians.

The text of Logan's "Speech to Lord Dunmore" is taken from Thomas Jefferson's "Notes on Virginia," Albert Ellery Bergh (ed.), *The Writings of Thomas Jefferson* (Washington, D.C.: The Thomas Jefferson Memorial Association, 1903), Vol. II, p. 89. Some twenty-three years after the event Jefferson prepared an extensive narrative concerning the text and the circumstances of the speech. He also provided affidavits from persons who had witnessed or heard contemporary accounts of the "transaction." In his narrative, Jefferson observed (*op. cit.*, pp. 304–5): "In order to make it intelligible to the reader, the transaction, on which it was founded, was stated, as it had been generally related in America at the time, and as I had heard it myself, in the circle of Lord Dunmore, and the officers who accompanied him; and the speech itself was given as it had, ten years before the printing of that book, circulated in the newspapers through all the then colonies, through the magazines of Great Britain, and periodical publications of Europe."

The Occasion

In the Spring of 1774, Indians and white men in the Ohio Valley played out in Lord Dunmore's War a tragedy that had been witnessed before, and would be witnessed again, as the red men confronted the white in North America. In some circumstances the war bears a striking resemblance to the hostilities between the Nez Perce Indians and the white settlers in the great Northwest a century later. Perhaps the only feature quite unique to Lord Dunmore's War was the interest maintained in it and in Logan, the Mingo chief, by Thomas Jefferson.

Endeavoring to counter the hypothesis of M. de Buffon and others that something in the conditions of life in North America caused animals (including man) to degenerate, Jefferson sought evidence to demonstrate that nothing in the environment doomed Americans to be inferior to Europeans. Jefferson found one of his proofs in the art of oratory, notably in the speech addressed by Logan, the Mingo chief, to Lord Dunmore, the Governor of Virginia. Of this speech, Jefferson declared that it "may challenge the whole orations of Demosthenes and Cicero, and of any more eminent orator, if Europe has furnished more eminent. . . ." [1]

The occasion for Lord Dunmore's War is epitomized in Logan's speech. Logan, taught by the followers of William Penn, was indeed the friend of the white men; and, like many another Indian friend of the white men, he lived to learn that white men are not all alike, that some of them said, "The only good Indian is a dead Indian." The degree of Captain Cresap's complicity in the murder of Logan's family is in dispute. Whether he participated in the act, or ordered it, or condoned

[1] Thomas Jefferson, *op. cit.*, pp. 87–88.

it, or merely failed to prevent it, will perhaps never be known; but it is established that Logan's people were indiscriminately slain by white men in retaliation for thefts committed by some Indians. Logan, in turn, sought vengeance against his former friends in the conflict generally known as Lord Dunmore's War.

Lord Dunmore, in 1774 the colonial Governor of Virginia, led a column of troops into Logan's homeland along the Ohio and Scioto rivers and sent another column under Andrew Lewis in a campaign in which the Indians were decisively defeated and sued for peace. So strong was Chief Logan's antipathy against his former friends that he personally refused to participate in the negotiations. Not wishing, however, to jeopardize the making of a treaty he absented himself from the council and instead sent a messenger charged with delivering the eloquent speech explaining why Logan could never make peace with the Virginians. The speech, immediately famous in its own right, has survived also because of the value placed upon it by Thomas Jefferson.

Logan served with the British forces during the American revolution until his death in 1780.

The Speech

SPEECH TO LORD DUNMORE

I appeal to any white man to say, if ever he entered Logan's cabin hungry, and he gave him not meat; if ever he came cold and naked, and he clothed him not. During the course of the last long and bloody war Logan remained idle in his cabin, an advocate for peace. Such was my love for the whites, that my countrymen pointed as they passed, and said, "Logan is the friend of white men." I had even thought to have lived with you, but for the injuries of one man. Colonel Cresap, the last spring, in cold blood, and unprovoked, murdered all the relations of Logan, not even sparing my women and children. There runs not a drop of my blood in the veins of any living creature. This called on me for revenge. I have sought it: I have killed many: I have fully glutted my vengeance: for my country I rejoice at the beams of peace. But do not harbor a thought that

*mine is the joy of fear. Logan never felt fear. He will not turn
on his heel to save his life. Who is there to mourn for Logan?
—Not one.*

Further Reading

Many pertinent facts concerning James Logan (Tahgahjute)
are lost in obscurity or tangled in controversy. Reuben Gold
Thwaites and Louise Phelps Kellogg (eds.), *Documentary History of Dunmore's War* (Madison: Wisconsin Historical Society,
1905) contains a brief account (pp. 305–306) concerning Logan's life, in addition to sources concerning Lord Dunmore's
War. Theodore Roosevelt, *The Winning of the West* (New York:
G. P. Putnam's Sons, 1895) contains (Vol. I, pp. 237–238) a
text of Logan's speech with an account of the circumstances
tending to absolve Cresap. Inasmuch as Thomas Jefferson is
largely responsible for the preservation of the Logan story, his
account is indispensable: Thomas Jefferson, "Notes on Virginia,"
in Albert Ellery Bergh (ed.), *The Writings of Thomas Jefferson*
(Washington, D.C.: The Thomas Jefferson Memorial Association, 1903). See Vol. II, pp. 1–261, and Appendix, pp. 263–329.

CHAPTER 2

On Signing the Constitution

BENJAMIN FRANKLIN

*. . . having lived long, I have experienced many
instances of being obliged, by better information
or fuller consideration, to change opinions even on
important subjects, which I once thought right,
but found to be otherwise.*

—BENJAMIN FRANKLIN

The Speaker

BENJAMIN FRANKLIN, one of the most famous Americans,
was born in Boston in 1706. On quarreling with his brother,
James, to whom he was apprenticed as a printer, he left Boston
for Philadelphia (1723) and for London (1724–26). In 1729 he
took a post with *The Pennsylvania Gazette,* of which he became editor and publisher in 1730. Thereafter his career was
marked by the thrift, enterprise, and common sense that have
long been considered Yankee, if not American, traits, and by
a civic spirit that led him to take part in establishing the American Philosophical Society, an academy (later the University of
Pennsylvania), and a library. He was the delegate from Pennsylvania to the Albany Congress of the colonies in 1754. While
urging moderation, he consistently supported the prerogatives of
the colonies against the British. When the break came between

Britain and America, he supported the colonies, even though his son, William Franklin, was a leader of the Tories. He was a delegate to the Continental Congress, a member of the committee to draft the Declaration of Independence (which he signed), and American commissioner to France, where his services as a diplomat were noteworthy. He represented the Americans in the negotiations that led to the treaty of peace. On his return to America (1785) he was made President of the Council of Pennsylvania and as delegate to the Constitutional Convention (1787) performed his last great service to his countrymen. He died in 1790, universally respected as statesman, scientist, and philosopher.

The text of Benjamin Franklin's speech "On Signing the Constitution" is taken from John Bigelow (ed.), *The Complete Works of Benjamin Franklin* . . . (New York: G. P. Putnam's Sons, 1888), Vol. IX, pp. 431–33.

The Occasion

Benjamin Franklin was the first man, as Alexander Hamilton was the second, to catch the vision of an American nation. Native of Boston, resident of Philadelphia, visitor in London and Paris, citizen of the world, Franklin was able without neglecting his obligations to his own Commonwealth of Pennsylvania to foresee the larger Commonwealth of America. His disposition toward American union was revealed in 1754, when at the Albany Congress he gained the acceptance of the representatives of seven British colonies in North America for his Plan of Union, only to see it refused by the colonial legislatures. Thirty-three years later, however, when fifty-five representatives of the several American commonwealths met at Philadelphia to consider another plan of union, Franklin's conceptions found a more favorable climate of opinion.

The draft of the Constitution read to the delegates in convention on September 17, 1787, was the result of debates—sometimes heated—that had taken place throughout the summer. The political genius of the American people—indeed of the human race—has never been more marked than in the deliberations of that convention. Confronted with a variety of vexed questions, of which any one could have thrown the convention into disorder and destroyed the hope of nationhood, the delegates demonstrated in holding fast to principle, while yielding in good spirit to compromises necessary to the common welfare, a capacity for self-government more often admired by than witnessed in humankind.

Alexander Hamilton, in the first number of *The Federalist*, with characteristic prescience explained the significance of the American endeavor:

After an unequivocal experience of the inefficacy of the subsisting Federal Government, you are called upon to deliberate on a new Constitution for the United States of America. The subject speaks its own importance; comprehending in its consequences, nothing less than the existence of the UNION, the safety and welfare of the parts of which it is composed, the fate of an empire, in many respects, the most interesting the world. It has been frequently remarked, that it seems to have been reserved to the people of this country, by their conduct and example, to decide the important question, whether societies of men are really capable or not, of establishing good government from re f[l]ection and choice, or whether they are forever destined to depend, for their political constitutions, on accident and force. If there be any truth in the remark, the crisis, at which we are arrived, may with propriety be regarded as the æra in which that decision is to be made; and a wrong election of the part we shall act, may, in this view, deserve to be considered as the general misfortune of mankind.[1]

Both George Washington and Alexander Hamilton brought high prestige to the convention in Philadelphia. As Moderator, Washington insured decorum, even as the delegates expressed strong differences of opinion; and Franklin, one may suppose, extended his influence throughout, as he did in his speech on September 17, 1787, for conciliation. Although Franklin, whose home was in Philadelphia, had faithfully attended the sessions of the Convention, he had not otherwise taken an active part in the deliberations. Past eighty years old, and not in abundant health and strength, he had let his presence and occasional remarks suffice. His major contribution to the joint enterprise was surely his moving the adoption of the draft of the constitution

[1] Harold C. Syrett and Jacob Cooke (eds.), *The Papers of Alexander Hamilton* (New York: Columbia University Press, 1962), Vol. IV, pp. 301–302.

as it had been framed for reference to the several legislatures, and his speech (here presented) in which he urged every member to sign and support the document. For it must be remembered that although the draft constitution was ready for presentation, it still had to receive approval of at least nine legislatures in order to take effect; and Franklin had experienced a generation earlier the disappointment of seeing his Plan of Union adopted by convention only to be defeated by legislature.

According to James Madison's notes of the Philadelphia Convention, after Benjamin Franklin's speech had been read in his behalf by James Wilson, also a delegate from Pennsylvania, and as the delegates were affixing their signatures to the document, Franklin looked toward the President's chair, on which a rising sun had been painted, and remarked to those delegates near him that artists have some difficulty in distinguishing a rising sun from a setting sun. "I have," said he, "often and often, in the course of the session, and the vicissitudes of my hopes and fears as to its issue, looked at that behind the President, without being able to tell whether it was rising or setting; but now at length, I have the happiness to know, that it is a rising, and not a setting sun." [2]

Presumably few men today would differ with the views of Franklin, and few would differ with the judgment that his speech delivered on September 17, 1787, is a veritable model of that quiet and reasoned eloquence, sometimes underestimated, that constrains to agreement the minds of judicious men.

The Speech

ON SIGNING THE CONSTITUTION

Mr. President:—I confess that I do not entirely approve of this Constitution at present; but, sir, I am not sure I shall never approve it; for, having lived long, I have experienced many instances of being obliged, by better information or fuller consideration, to change opinions even on important subjects, which I once thought right, but found to be otherwise. It is therefore

---

[2] E. H. Scott, ed., *Journal of the Constitutional Convention Kept by James Madison* (Chicago: Scott, Foresman and Co., 1893), p. 763.

that, the older I grow, the more apt I am to doubt my own judgment of others. Most men, indeed, as well as most sects in religion, think themselves in possession of all truth, and that wherever others differ from them, it is so far error. Steele, a Protestant, in a dedication, tells the Pope that the only difference between our two churches in their opinions of the certainty of their doctrine is, the Romish Church is infallible, *and the Church of England is* never in the wrong. *But though many private persons think almost as highly of their own infallibility as that of their sect, few express it so naturally as a certain French lady, who, in a little dispute with her sister, said: "But I meet with nobody but myself that is* always in the right." "Je ne trouve que moi qui aie toujours raison."

In these sentiments, sir, I agree to this Constitution, with all its faults—if they are such;—because I think a general government necessary for us, and there is no form of government but what may be a blessing to the people, if well administered; and I believe further, that this is likely to be well administered for a course of years, and can only end in despotism, as other forms have done before it, when the people shall become so corrupted as to need despotic government, being incapable of any other. I doubt, too, whether any other convention we can obtain, may be able to make a better Constitution; for, when you assemble a number of men, to have the advantage of their joint wisdom, you inevitably assemble with those men, all their prejudices, their passions, their errors of opinion, their local interests, and their selfish views. From such an assembly can a perfect *production be expected? It therefore astonishes me, sir, to find this system approaching so near to perfection as it does; and I think it will astonish our enemies, who are waiting with confidence to hear that our counsels are confounded like those of the builders of Babel, and that our States are on the point of separation, only to meet hereafter for the purpose of cutting one another's throats. Thus I consent, sir, to this Constitution, because I expect no better, and because I am not sure that it is not the best. The opinions I have had of its* errors *I sacrifice to the public good. I have never whispered a syllable of them abroad. Within these walls they were born, and here they shall die. If every one of us, in returning to our constituents, were to report the objections he has had to it, and endeavor to gain partisans in support of them, we might prevent its being generally received, and thereby lose all the salutary effects and great advantages resulting naturally in our favor among foreign nations, as well as among ourselves, from our real or apparent unanimity. Much of the strength and efficiency of any government in procuring and securing happiness to the people, depends on* opinion, *on the general opinion, of the goodness of that government, as well·as of the wisdom and integrity of its governors. I hope, therefore, for our own sakes, as a part of the people, and for the sake of our posterity, that we shall act heartily and unanimously in recommending this Constitution, wherever our influence may extend, and turn our future thoughts and endeavors to the means of having it* well administered.

On the whole, sir, I cannot help expressing a wish that every member of the convention who may still have objections to it would with me on this occasion doubt a little of his own infallibility, and, to make manifest *our* unanimity, *put his name to this instrument.*

Further Reading

Anyone could spend a lifetime in reading the materials in and out of print concerning either of two fascinating subjects: the life of Benjamin Franklin, and the formation of the Constitution of the United States. When the two fascinating subjects are conjoined, recommendations for reading must be governed by the expedient question: What sources are readily available in convenient form?

The standard treatment of the formation of the Constitution is Max Farrand's *The Framing of the Constitution of the United States* (New Haven: Yale University Press, 1913), which may be consulted along with the authoritative work edited by Farrand, *The Records of the Federal Convention of 1787* (New Haven: Yale University Press, 1911–1937), 4 vols. For some students perhaps a more convenient source will be found in *The Federal Convention and the Formation of the Union of the American States* (New York: The Liberal Arts Press, 1958), edited by Winton U. Solberg with the acknowledged purpose to "illustrate the role of the Federal Convention in the formation of the American Constitution."

Reading about Franklin might well begin with *The Autobiography of Benjamin Franklin,* which has been translated into many languages, published in countless editions, and read with delight and perhaps with edification by millions of persons. Certainly one of the most influential books ever written by an American, it is now available in a handsome new edition edited by Leonard W. Labaree and colleagues and published (1964) by the Yale University Press. *The Papers of Benjamin Franklin* (New Haven: Yale University Press, 1959) is being published serially under the editorship of Leonard Labaree and staff, with the counsel of an administrative board, an editorial advisory committee, and a cooperating committee. Volume I (1959) covers the period from January 6, 1706, through December 31, 1734. The successive issues to Volume X (1966) include documents and correspondence through December 31, 1763.

Among the many other books concerning Franklin, the following may be suggested as convenient, reliable, and readable: Herbert W. Schneider (ed.), *Benjamin Franklin: The Autobiography and Selections from His Other Writings* (New York: The Liberal Arts Press, 1952); Frank Luther Mott and Chester E. Jorgenson (eds.), *Benjamin Franklin: Representative Selections, with Introduction, Bibliography and Notes* (New York: American Book Company, 1936); Carl Van Doren, *Benjamin Franklin's Autobiographical Writings* (New York: The Viking Press, 1945); and Bernard Faÿ, *Benjamin Franklin: The Apostle of Modern Times* (Boston: Little, Brown and Co., 1929).

CHAPTER 3

To Free the Slaves

JOHN BROWN

*I say I am yet too young to understand that
God is any respecter of persons.*

—JOHN BROWN

The Speaker

JOHN BROWN, known in abolitionist tracts as "Old Brown of
Osawatomie," was born in Torrington, Connecticut, on May 9,
1800, and was hanged at Charlestown, Virginia, on December
2, 1859. He spent the years intervening in Ohio, Pennsylvania,
Massachusetts, and New York. He was consistently unfortunate
in business enterprises. Nevertheless he married twice and
fathered twenty children, of whom five sons went with him to
Kansas in 1855 to help defeat pro-slavery forces and maintain
Kansas as a free state. In his campaign to keep Kansas free,
he led a band that deliberately killed five pro-slavery settlers
in a community on the Pottawatomie River. He received national
recognition for this and other exploits against slavery. Determined to extend his activities, he began in 1857 to plan a project
to free slaves. At a convention held in Ontario, Canada, in 1858,
he enlisted men for the assault on the "slave power." In 1859
he rented a farm near Harpers Ferry, Virginia (now West Virginia), and on October 16, 1859, with 21 followers he attacked

and captured the United States Arsenal. He took a number of prisoners, including Col. Lewis Washington.

Brown apparently had no well-concerted plan of action, but depended on a slave uprising that did not occur. On the morning after the capture of the arsenal, a company of United States Marines under the command of Col. Robert E. Lee defeated Brown's force and retook the arsenal. Ten of Brown's men were killed, and he was wounded. The attack on the arsenal aroused fears of servile insurrection throughout the South and exposed the rift in opinion between conservatives and abolitionists in the North.

The text of John Brown's speech of November 2, 1859, prior to his execution on December 2, 1859, is taken from *Harper's Weekly,* Vol. III, No. 150 (November 12, 1859), p. 726.

The Occasion

When John Brown transferred his activities from the border states of Kansas and Missouri to Virginia, he set in motion a train of events that seemed, like a tragic drama, to move inexorably toward a set conclusion.[1] Whether the conflict that ensued was indeed irrepressible, as has been maintained, is beyond knowledge; but once John Brown had resorted to violence in an effort to encourage a servile rebellion in Virginia—a state whose inhabitants had memories of Nat Turner, the slave who led the Southampton Insurrection in 1831—the die was cast. Moreover, Virginians, like other Southerners, were prepared to believe the worst of the despised Yankees; and they were not comforted by Northern expressions of sympathy for John Brown. In 1862, John Esten Cooke, a private in the Richmond Howitzers, wrote a perceptive account of the immediate effect of John Brown's incursion into Virginia:

The outrage so lately perpetrated upon the soil of Virginia awakened the most intense apprehensions for the safety of the Union in the minds of every lover of his country. But, perhaps, the most striking

[1] This statement concerning John Brown's speech at Charlestown, Virginia, is based on newspaper accounts of the raid and ensuing events and on the sources listed in the section on further reading.

results of it were the immediate development of a sympathy for Old Brown and his associates which the Northern people could not conceal, and of a corresponding indignation on the part of the Southern people at the unparalleled insult offered to them and their institutions, and of their determination, at all hazards, to avenge it. An immediate impetus was given to the military spirit of the South, with a view to prepare for the events which must surely come. New companies were enrolled, not only in the city of Richmond and in the State of Virginia, but like activity was observable as extending throughout the whole South.

Old Brown had been tried by a jury of his peers, and, as he richly deserved, had been sentenced to be hanged on the 2d day of December, and following his trial came those of the conspirators, and with a like result. The abolition newspapers of the North were unblushing in expressing their sympathy for these wretches, and when it was at last ascertained that none but the most insane could entertain hopes of a pardon to them, their rescue from the clutches of the law was advocated with the most insolent boldness.[2]

The trial of John Brown was high drama in which he was the leading actor conscious of his role. His part in the drama surely contributed to the bloodshed he predicted.[3] His decorum, his self-assurance, his courage, and not least his eloquence moved men both North and South, albeit to different conclusions. In keeping with the differing opinions concerning John Brown, the accounts of his final speech do not agree.

James Redpath, writing shortly after the event, declared:

During the absence of the Jury in Coppoc's case, in order that no time should be wasted, John Brown was brought in from jail to be sentenced. He walked with considerable difficulty, and every movement appeared to be attended with pain, although his features gave no expression of it. It was late, and the gaslights gave an almost deathly pallor to his face. He seated himself near his counsel, and, after once resting his head upon his right hand, remained entirely motionless, and for a time appeared unconscious of all that passed around—especially unconscious of the execrations audibly whispered

[2] Richard B. Harwell, "A Note on John Brown," p. 9.

[3] As John Brown left his cell on the way to the gallows, he handed to a bystander a paper bearing the following message: "I John Brown am now quite *certain* that the crimes of this *guilty land: will* never be purged *away;* but with Blood. I had *as I now think: vainly* flattered myself that without *very much* bloodshed; it might be done." From photocopy of the original in Villard, *John Brown: 1800–1859* . . . , facing p. 554.

by spectators: "D——d black-hearted villain– heart as black as a stove-pipe–" and many such. While the Judge read his decision on the points of exception which had been submitted, Brown sat very firm, with lips tightly compressed, but with no appearance of affectation of stern-ness. He was like a block of stone. When the clerk directed him to stand and say why sentence should not be passed upon him, he rose and leaned slightly forward, his hands resting on the table. He spoke timidly—hesitatingly, indeed—and in a voice singularly gentle and mild. But his sentences came confused from his mouth, and he seemed to be wholly unprepared to speak at this time. Types can give no in-timation of the soft and tender tones, yet calm and manly withal, that filled the Court room, and, I think, touched the hearts of many who had come only to rejoice at the heaviest blow their victim was to suffer.[4]

Writing some fifty years after the event, Oswald Garrison Villard gives a somewhat different impression of John Brown's manner and delivery:

Again there was a thrill in the crowded court-room, when the clerk asked John Brown whether he had anything to say why sentence should not be pronounced upon him. And well the crowd might be stirred, for what it was now to hear from the lips of the man for whose life it thirsted must forever remain on the list of great American speeches,[5] an utterance worthy not merely of the man who voiced it, but of the mighty cause of human freedom for which he struck so pow-erful a blow. Drawing himself up to his full stature, with flashing eagle eyes and calm, clear and distinct tones, John Brown again addressed, not the men who surrounded him, but the whole body of his country-men, North, South, East and West.[6]

A third account by an eyewitness, Judge Thomas Russell, in-dicated that John Brown

[4] James Redpath, *The Public Life of Capt. John Brown* . . . , pp. 339–40.

[5] "His brief speech at Gettysburg will not easily be surpassed by words on any recorded occasion. This and one other American speech, that of John Brown to the court that tried him, and a part of Kossuth's speech at Birming-ham, can only be compared with each other, and with no fourth,"—said Ralph Waldo Emerson, at the funeral services for Abraham Lincoln, held in Concord, April 19, 1865. Oswald Garrison Villard, *op. cit.* (1910 edition), pp. 497–98.

[6] *Ibid.*, p. 646.

. . . delivered the remarkable speech which you have just read, speaking with perfect calmness of voice and mildness of manner, winning the respect of all for his courage and firmness. His self-possession was wonderful, because his sentence, at this time, was unexpected, and his remarks were entirely unprepared.[7]

One need not agree with any of the estimates of John Brown's speech, nor determine whether Emerson was sound in his critical judgments, nor even reach a conclusion concerning the vexed question of Brown's sanity in order to observe that his short speech at Charlestown, Virginia, was profoundly influential. Brown's devotion to his fixed idea, and his eloquence, derived from an unshakable personal commitment demonstrated both by a willingness to hazard his own life and to kill other men, have set him apart even a century later as one who released power to be reckoned with. Fifty years after Brown's death, W. E. Burghardt Du Bois analyzed John Brown's life force from the point of view of the Negro American:

John Brown worked not simply for Black Men—he worked with them; and he was a companion of their daily life, knew their faults and virtues, and felt, as few white Americans have felt, the bitter tragedy of their lot.[8]

John Brown, said Du Bois, "of all Americans has perhaps come nearest to touching the real souls of black folk." [9] Perhaps the marching song of some of the Union troops in the Civil War is relevant today:

> "John Brown's body is moldering in the ground,
> But his soul is marching on.
> Glory, Hallelujah!" [10]

The Speech

TO FREE THE SLAVES

I have, may it please the Court, a few words to say. In the first place, I deny every thing but what I have all along ad-

[7] *Ibid.*, p. 498.
[8] W. E. Burghardt Du Bois, *John Brown*, p. 8.
[9] *Ibid.*, p. 9.
[10] William Elsey Connelley, *John Brown*, p. 392.

mitted, of a design on my part to free slaves. I intended, certainly, to have made a clean thing of that matter, as I did last winter, when I went into Missouri, and there took slaves without the snapping of a gun on either side, moving them through the country, and finally leaving them in Canada. I designed to have done the same thing again on a larger scale. That was all I intended. I never did intend murder or treason, or the destruction of property, or to excite or incite slaves to rebellion, or to make insurrection. I have another objection, and that is that it is unjust that I should suffer such a penalty. Had I interfered in the manner in which I admit, and which I admit had been fairly proved—for I admire the truthfulness and candor of the greater portion of the witnesses who have testified in this case—had I so interfered in behalf of the rich, the powerful, the intelligent, the so-called great, or in behalf of any of their friends, either father, mother, brother, sister, wife, or children, or any of that class, and suffered and sacrificed what I have in this interference, it would have been all right; every man in this court would have deemed it an act worthy of reward rather than punishment.

An Appeal to the Bible

This Court acknowledges, too, as I suppose, the validity of the law of God. I see a book kissed, which I suppose to be the Bible, or at least the New Testament, which teaches me that all things whatsoever I would that men should do to me I should do even so to them. It teaches me, further, to remember them that are in bonds as bound with them. I endeavored to act up to that instruction. I say I am yet too young to understand that God is any respecter of persons. I believe that to have interfered as I have done, as I have always freely admitted I have done, in behalf of His despised poor, is no wrong, but right. Now, if it is deemed necessary that I should forfeit my life for the furtherance of the ends of justice, and mingle my blood further with the blood of my children and with the blood of millions in this slave country, whose rights are disregarded by wicked, cruel, and unjust enactments, I say let it be done. Let me say one word further. I feel entirely satisfied with the treatment I have received on my trial. Considering all the circumstances, it has been more generous than I expected; but I feel no consciousness of guilt. I have stated from the first what was my intention and what was not. I never had any design against the liberty of any person, nor any disposition to commit treason or incite slaves to rebel or make any general insurrection. I never encouraged any man to do so, but always discouraged any idea of that kind. Let me say, also, in regard to the statements made by some of those who were connected with me: I fear it has been stated by some of them that I have induced them to join me, but the contrary is true. I do not say this to injure them, but as regretting their weakness. Not one joined me but of his own accord, and the greater part at their own expense. A number of them I never saw and never had a word of conversation with till the day they came to me, and that was for the purpose I have stated. Now I have done.

Further Reading

The materials concerning John Brown and the raid on Harpers Ferry are for the most part highly partisan, thus reflecting the divisions of thought and feeling created in December, 1859. Robert Penn Warren suggests that Oswald Garrison Villard, in *John Brown: 1800–1859: A Biography Fifty Years After* (Boston: Houghton Mifflin Co., 1910) is not sufficiently objective. In the new and revised edition of his work (New York: Alfred A. Knopf, 1943) based on new information concerning the Kansas murders Villard offers some judgments that would seem to relieve him of the onus suggested by Warren. Hill Peebles Wilson, in *John Brown: Soldier of Fortune: A Critique* (Lawrence, Kansas: Hill P. Wilson, 1913) is even more severe than Warren in his criticism of Villard. Whatever limitations of prejudice may be ascribed to the work of Oswald Garrison Villard, his book—in the editions of 1910 and 1943—represents a highly significant contribution to the John Brown story. The systematic bibliography (pp. 689–709 in the 1910 edition) is enough to justify the book.

Of the earlier treatises, the most useful, despite its partisanship, is doubtless James Redpath's *The Public Life of Capt.*

John Brown with an Auto-Biography of His Childhood and Youth (Boston: Thayer and Eldridge, 1860). Other works that may be mentioned are William Elsey Connelley's *John Brown* (Topeka, Kansas: Crane & Co., 1900); F. B. Sanborn's *The Life and Letters of John Brown: Liberator of Kansas, and Martyr of Virginia* (Concord, Massachusetts: F. B. Sanborn, 1910); and Richard J. Hinton's *John Brown and His Men With Some Account of the Roads They Traveled to Reach Harper's Ferry*, rev. ed. (New York: Funk & Wagnalls Co., n.d.).

John Brown (Philadelphia: George W. Jacobs & Co., 1909), by W. E. Burghardt Du Bois, is noteworthy in its presentation of the special point of view of the Negro toward John Brown. Richard B. Harwell's perceptive "A Note on John Brown" appears in *A Check List of an Exhibition of John Brown: 1800–1859 and A Note on John Brown* (Lawrence: University of Kansas Libraries, 1959). Some of the primary source materials for the raid on Harpers Ferry can be found conveniently in Edward Stone (ed.), *Incident at Harper's Ferry* (Englewood Cliffs, New Jersey: Prentice-Hall, Inc., 1956).

CHAPTER 4

The Gettysburg Address

ABRAHAM LINCOLN

It is for us, the living, rather to be dedicated here to the unfinished work that they have thus far so nobly carried on.

—ABRAHAM LINCOLN

The Speaker

ABRAHAM LINCOLN, sixteenth President of the United States, was born on February 12, 1809, in Hardin County, Kentucky. He was the son of Thomas Lincoln, a frontier farmer, and of Nancy Hanks, who died in 1818. Thomas Lincoln then married Sarah Bush Johnston.

Thomas Lincoln moved his family from Kentucky to Indiana and thence, in 1830, to Illinois. The young Lincoln settled in New Salem, a village near Springfield, where he kept a store, ran a mill, split rails, and did odd jobs. At one point he served as postmaster, and during the Black Hawk War he was chosen captain of a volunteer company. On his own, Lincoln studied law and surveying. In 1834 he was elected to the Illinois State Legislature, of which he was a member until 1841. He was licensed as an attorney in 1836 and began the practice of law in Springfield as the partner first of J. T. Stuart and later of Stephen Logan and William H. Herndon.

On his marriage to Mary Todd in 1842, Lincoln settled down to the practice of law and achieved local prominence as a successful attorney and personal popularity as a man of probity and an inimitable story-teller. He was elected to the Congress of the United States, in which he served one term (1847–1848). His forthright opposition to the Mexican War was unpopular and he was not returned. In 1854 and thereafter he opposed Stephen A. Douglas and the Kansas-Nebraska Bill. In 1856 he became a member of the new Republican party and two years later was nominated by the Republican Party to run against Douglas for the United States Senate. His nomination, and the ensuing debates with Douglas, brought Lincoln into nation-wide prominence as an opponent of slavery, and his stature was further enhanced, following his defeat by Douglas, by his speech (1860) at the Cooper Union in New York. In 1860 Lincoln was nominated and elected to the Presidency of the United States. His election was the ostensible reason for the secession of the southern states and the establishment of the Confederacy. As president of a nation at war with itself, Lincoln maintained a policy of firm support of the Union and denied the right of the states to secede. He demonstrated the courage, persistence, humanity, and wisdom that have contributed to the Lincoln legend and placed him first in the affections of many Americans and indeed of men throughout the world. Near the successful conclusion of the Civil War, on April 14, 1865, he was assassinated by John Wilkes Booth. The Lincoln tomb is at Springfield, Illinois.

The text of Abraham Lincoln's Address at Gettysburg is taken from "Dedicatory Address of President Lincoln," in *Edward Everett at Gettysburg* (Boston: Massachusetts Historical Society, 1963), p. 11.

The Occasion

The Gettysburg Address demonstrates some of the difficulties of rhetorical criticism.[1] Testimony can be brought to bear to

[1] This statement concerning Abraham Lincoln and the Gettysburg Address is drawn from, among others, the sources listed in the section on further reading.

prove that the speech was received with prolonged applause or with perfunctory applause, or with no applause at all. Evidence can be adduced to prove that the speech was read, that it was spoken without the use of a manuscript, or that it was delivered with slight reference to a manuscript. Witnesses attest variously that the speech received close attention, or that the hearers had just begun to follow the speech when they were astonished to discover that the speaker had concluded. The reports and editorial judgments that appeared in the newspapers following the speech are similarly inconclusive. In general criticism tended to follow the lines of partisanship. Even the text of the speech as uttered, rather than as approved by Lincoln after the event, is in doubt in minor particulars. No electronic devices recorded what Lincoln had to say, and stenographers did not hear or transcribe with perfect agreement!

Fortunately, however, some facts can be established to the satisfaction of the most captious critic:

1. The address was delivered on November 19, 1863.

2. In keeping with Lincoln's practice concerning major pronouncements during his presidency, the Gettysburg Address was prepared in writing in advance.

3. The address was delivered out-of-doors on the site of the great battle of Gettysburg which had been fought during the first three days of the previous July.

4. The ostensible purpose of the speech was to dedicate a national cemetery.

5. A large audience, perhaps as many as 18,000 people, attended.

6. In the audience, included in the platform party, were the leading members of Lincoln's administration.

7. Lincoln had a high tenor speaking voice which could be heard at a great distance.

8. President Lincoln's "remarks" followed the formal dedicatory address by Edward Everett, the designated "Orator of the Day."

William E. Barton, who conscientiously endeavored to find and assess the evidence concerning the Gettysburg Address, thought the Honorable Wayne MacVeagh, later Attorney General of the United States, to be one of the most competent of the persons who heard the Address. MacVeagh wrote:

As he came forward he seemed to me, and I was sitting near to him, visibly to dominate the scene, and while over his plain and rugged countenance appeared to settle a great melancholy, it was somehow lightened by a great hope. As he began to speak I instinctively felt that the occasion was taking on a new grandeur, as of a great moment in history; and then there followed, in a slow and very impressive and far-reaching utterance, the words with which the whole world has long been familiar. As each word was spoken it appeared to me so clearly fraught with a message not only for us of his day, but for the untold generations of men, that before he concluded I found myself possessed of a reverential awe for its complete justification of the great war he was conducting, as if conducted, as in truth it was, in the interest of mankind. Surely at that moment he justified the inspired portraiture of Lowell in the "Commemoration Ode." [2]

Perhaps in Fletcher G. Ransom's painting the artist's eye has caught, and the artist's hands have recounted, the event as Mac-Veagh experienced it.[3]

The story of the Gettysburg Address does not end with its delivery on November 19, 1863. As David C. Mearns observed,

Mr. Lincoln is the most quotable notable in history. His writings constitute the American scriptures, the testaments of democracy, the trade-marks of tradition, the prescriptions of the patriots.[4]

Lincoln's speeches are the most significant elements in his discourse. The Gettysburg Address is doubtless the most widely known of all Lincoln's speeches and writings. J. G. Randall thought it marked a climax in Lincoln's thought of America's larger role. In Lincoln's career, Randall observed, there is something to be studied as a proof of the meaning and opportunity of democracy.[5]

If one were required to choose from the whole body of American literature the single work most widely known, most universally accepted as characteristic of American discourse at its best, that work would doubtless be not a poem, nor an essay, nor a novel. It would be the three-minute speech that Abraham Lincoln delivered at Gettysburg. That Lincoln, the child of the

[2] William E. Barton, *Lincoln at Gettysburg* . . . , pp. 184–85.
[3] See the frontispiece to this volume.
[4] David C. Mearns, in the introduction to Archer H. Shaw, *The Lincoln Encyclopedia* . . . , p. vii.
[5] J. G. Randall, *Lincoln the President: Springfield to Gettysburg*, p. xi.

forest and the prairies, without formal education worth mentioning, without the advantages of wealth or social position, should have learned to govern a nation, and to command armies, is remarkable. That he taught himself to speak the English language so well as to gain the commendation of scholars for his mastery of the English sounds, the English sentence, is no less remarkable.

It is noteworthy that when Professor Lane Cooper came to choose a speech to be presented in the introduction to his translation of Aristotle's *Rhetoric*, he chose the Gettysburg Address. "This celebrated speech," he said, "is a good hunting-ground for illustrations of Aristotle's *Rhetoric;* so good, in fact, that a complete analysis of the speech by his principles would here be unwieldy." [6] On contemplation some would say that even more remarkable than Abraham Lincoln's command of armies or of governments was his command of the English language.

The Speech

THE GETTYSBURG ADDRESS (DEDICATORY ADDRESS OF PRESIDENT LINCOLN)

Fourscore and seven years ago our fathers brought forth upon this continent a new nation, conceived in Liberty, and dedicated to the proposition that all men are created equal.

Now we are engaged in a great civil war, testing whether that nation, or any nation so conceived and so dedicated, can long endure. We are met on a great battle-field of that war. We are met to dedicate a portion of it as the final resting-place of those who here gave their lives that that nation might live. It is altogether fitting and proper that we should do this.

But in a larger sense we cannot dedicate, we cannot consecrate, we cannot hallow this ground. The brave men, living and dead, who struggled here, have consecrated it far above our power to add or detract. The world will little note nor long

---

[6] Lane Cooper, (ed.), *The Rhetoric of Aristotle* (New York: Appleton-Century-Crofts, 1932), p. xxxi.

remember what we say here, but it can never forget what they did here. It is for us, the living, rather to be dedicated here to the unfinished work that they have thus far so nobly carried on. It is rather for us to be here dedicated to the great task remaining before us—that from these honored dead we take increased devotion to the cause for which they here gave the last full measure of devotion—that we here highly resolve that the dead shall not have died in vain; that the nation shall, under God, have a new birth of freedom, and that the government of the people, by the people, and for the people, shall not perish from the earth.

Further Reading

The texts of Lincoln's speeches will be found in Roy P. Basler (ed.), *The Collected Works of Abraham Lincoln* (New Brunswick, New Jersey: Rutgers University Press, 1953) 8 vols. Except for those who must have the convenience of a single volume, this edition supersedes *Abraham Lincoln: His Speeches and Writings* (Cleveland: The World Publishing Co., 1946) also edited by Roy P. Basler.

In the mountains of materials concerning Lincoln, it would appear that every aspect of his life has been covered. Perhaps the best approach to Lincoln is through the works of Sandburg and of Randall, as follows: Carl Sandburg, *Abraham Lincoln: The Prairie Years* (New York: Harcourt, Brace & Company, 1926), 2 vols.; Carl Sandburg, *Abraham Lincoln: The War Years* (New York: Harcourt, Brace & Company, 1939), 4 vols.; and J. G. Randall, *Lincoln the President,* published in four volumes (1945, 1945, 1952, and 1955) with various sub-titles by Dodd, Mead & Co., New York. The fourth volume is under the joint authorship of J. G. Randall and Richard N. Current.

A helpful guide through the maze of Lincolniana is Archer H. Shaw (ed.), *The Lincoln Encyclopedia: The Spoken and Written Words of Abraham Lincoln Arranged for Ready Reference* (New York: The Macmillan Co., 1950).

Critical analyses of Abraham Lincoln's career as a speech-maker are available in W. Norwood Brigance, *A History and Criticism of American Public Address* (New York: McGraw-

Hill Book Co., Inc., 1942), Vol. II. See "Abraham Lincoln: His Development in the Skills of the Platform," by Mildred Freburg Berry, and "Abraham Lincoln: His Emergence as the Voice of the People," by Earl W. Wiley. A selected bibliography (pp. 874–77) is provided.

"The Gettysburg Address" has been the subject of innumerable treatises of which no two seem to be entirely in accord. William E. Barton, *Lincoln at Gettysburg: What He Intended to Say; What He Said; What He Was Reported to Have Said; What He Wished He Had Said* (Indianapolis: The Bobbs-Merrill Co., 1930) undertakes to tell the whole story. The book also includes the text of the Address of the Honorable Edward Everett, who was announced as the orator of the day at the dedication. An exchange of letters between Everett and Lincoln, with a circumstantial account of the events of the dedication, appears in Paul Revere Frothingham, *Edward Everett: Orator and Statesman* (Boston: Houghton Mifflin Co. 1925).

CHAPTER 5

We Are Young No Longer
CHIEF SPOTTED TAIL

*Listen to the dirge of the dry leaves, that were
green and vigorous but a few moons before! We
are a part of this life and it seems that our time
is come.*

—CHIEF SPOTTED TAIL

The Speaker

SPOTTED TAIL (Sinte Galeska), described by historian George
E. Hyde as "probably the greatest Sioux chief of his period,"
was the recognized leader of the Brulés after the retirement
of Little Thunder around 1866. Among the Sioux and the white
men who dealt with Indians, Spotted Tail was highly respected
for bravery, for shrewdness, and for ripened wisdom. When he
became convinced that the Indian cause was hopeless and that
the tribes must eventually adapt themselves to the ways of white
men his efforts to foster peaceful relations made him the spokesman for the Indians who wanted peace. It also brought him
discredit among the militant groups. He was a less polished
orator than the Oglala Red Cloud, but he was known as an
effective speaker, and in dealing with white agents his ability
to reason logically and his sharp wit whittled from the government concessions that could not have been won by force.

37

The text for "We Are Young No Longer" is taken from Charles A. Eastman, *Indian Heroes and Great Chieftains* (Boston: Little, Brown and Co., 1918), pp. 35–36. Eastman, a Santee Sioux, reconstructed the speech in translation from the account given by Sioux with whom he was closely associated in his capacity as physician at the Pine Ridge Reservation. The second version is a poetic adaptation by John G. Neihardt in *The Song of the Indian Wars*, a part of the epic *Cycle of the West* (New York: The Macmillan Co., 1949), pp. 29–30. Reprinted by permission of the author.

The Occasion

American Indians, particularly the plains Indians, have been so variously stereotyped by observers, writers, and the mass media that it is difficult to think of them as people meeting the problems of living in a harsh world to which all races are subject. The image of the Indian as a shiftless, deceitful, sub-human creature, or a painted monster, invincible and demonic, or even as Rousseau's noble savage, does an injustice to the human qualities of the red man. A more reasonable assessment is contained in the words of Wendell Phillips as quoted by Jacob P. Dunn in *Massacres of the Mountains:*

From Massachusetts Bay back to their own hunting-grounds, every few miles is written down in imperishable record as a spot where the scanty, scattered tribes made a stand for justice and their own rights. Neither Greece, nor Germany, nor the French, nor the Scotch, can show a prouder record. And instead of searing it over with infamy and illustrated epithets, the future will recognize it as a glorious record of a race that never melted out and never died away, but stood up manfully, man by man, foot by foot, and fought it out for the land God gave him against the world, which seemed to be poured out over him.[1]

In the struggle to stand up manfully for justice and their rights, Indians, like white men, disagreed about the proper course to follow. They were not united, even in opposition to the whites, and the decisions for treaty or warpath were hammered out in council or negotiation. Among the Sioux, the war-

[1] (New York: Archer House, Inc.), p. 33.

like spirit was epitomized in the militant leader Red Cloud, the most powerful chief of the Oglalas and an orator famous for both passion and restraint in the articulation of his views. The outstanding spokesman for the advocates of peace was Spotted Tail. Until 1855 he had concurred in a war policy against the encroaching whites, but in the fall of that year he and a small group of warriors responsible for various depredations surrendered themselves to General Harney and went into captivity to prevent retaliation against the tribe. Expecting to be killed, the warriors rode in singing their death songs, but instead they were imprisoned at Fort Leavenworth and eventually pardoned. The two years of captivity wrought a change in Spotted Tail's thinking; his observations brought him to the conclusion that the Indians could not hope to hold back the tide of white men flowing into the country and that continued resistance could only prolong the suffering of survivors. His espousal of peace policy brought him into disfavor with the militant tribes and gave rise to the suggestion in many of the historical accounts that the Brulé chief was motivated by concern for his own safety. But Spotted Tail was no coward. As George E. Hyde somewhat heatedly points out, he fought white men and enemy Pawnees for a decade after 1855, and his personal bravery was never in question. Hyde attributes the aura of discredit surrounding Spotted Tail to the prolific accounts of Sioux events disseminating from the Oglala reservation at Pine Ridge, where Red Cloud was the hero and the long hairs tended to belittle Spotted Tail in order to aggrandize Red Cloud and Crazy Horse.[2] Spotted Tail's disaffection with prevailing sentiment may more properly be attributed to his generally conceded intelligence and foresight than to fear.

The speech by the Brulé chief here titled "We Are Young No Longer" is reported by Charles Eastman as presented in an Indian council in 1866. In the spring of that year a peace commission headed by E. B. Taylor of the United States Indian Office invited the Sioux of the Powder River area to a council at Fort Laramie, in southeast Wyoming. The commissioners hoped to negotiate a treaty granting rights to a new wagon

[2] George E. Hyde, *Spotted Tail's Folk: A History of the Brulé Sioux,* p. ix.

road through the Sioux hunting grounds. The council dissolved
when the inopportune arrival of Col. Henry B. Carrington with
a column of cavalry convinced the Indians that the white chiefs
intended to steal the road with or without a treaty; Red Cloud
made an impassioned speech of defiance and stalked out of the
council. Shortly afterward, according to Eastman, the Oglala
chief convened a council on the Powder River to consider policy; at this council Spotted Tail advocated peace in the speech
that follows.

The plea fell upon unreceptive ears, as Eastman described
the event. It set forth an unpopular view and presented facts
unpleasant to face at any time; but the excited state of mind
of the Sioux and their rage at the deceit practiced upon them
prepared sterile ground for an appeal to reason and a plea for
peace. Eastman describes the response as "ominous silence,"
without even the customary *How!* of assent.

The problems of both text and occasion are particularly difficult in this speech, aside from the uncertainties inherent in
dealing with translation. Even the facts of the occasion as given
by Eastman are disputed; Hyde dismisses the Powder River
Council as unlikely to have taken place at all and Spotted Tail's
participation as even more unlikely. He finds no evidence that
such a council was held.[3] Eastman's information, including the
texts of speeches, came from the Oglalas at Pine Ridge, with
whom he was intimately associated for some time. Whether
they misinformed him is a moot question; Indians had few
qualms about spinning yarns for white men, but Eastman was
not a white man; he was a Sioux like themselves. His appraisal
of Spotted Tail does not show the prejudice Hyde traced to
Pine Ridge influence; Eastman gives the Brulé due credit for
intelligence and foresight. Various inaccuracies of detail have
led historians to discount Eastman as a reliable source, but if
the Powder River council is fabrication, it represents a powerful imaginative effort, and the speeches of Sitting Bull, Red
Cloud and Spotted Tail as given by Eastman accord with the
known views of each man.

The second version of the speech, by the poet John G. Neihardt, affords an excellent example of the effective use to be
made of a speech in a literary work. He credits the story of

[3] *Ibid.,* pp. 117–118.

the council and the unenthusiastic reception of Spotted Tail's words. As used in the narrative, it provides a striking contrast to the fiery war talks by Red Cloud and Sitting Bull, and the adaptations Neihardt made to his verse form reveal the poet's sound rhetorical instincts. This version follows faithfully the substance of the speech, but sharpens the style and force with more concrete language, firmer verbs and nouns, and increased metaphor. Neihardt thought that except for rhyme and meter his adaptation might be closer to what Spotted Tail actually said; [4] because Eastman was translating into language white men would readily understand, he used abstract words and general statements that would probably have been concrete terms in the original. Where Eastman translates: ". . . yet he is so great and so flourishing that there must be some virtue and truth in his philosophy," for example, Neihardt puts the idea into concrete language:

> Something that is true
> Must help him do the things that he can do,
> For lies are not so mighty!

In the brief passages at the beginning and end, Neihardt heightens the drama by describing the listeners' unsympathetic response, elaborated from Eastman's brief comment to suggest that Spotted Tail recognized the futility of his appeal to wisdom.

Time has vindicated the judgment of Spotted Tail. Moderation and foresight are less spectacular than war cries, but courage takes many forms and does not necessarily lose in being quiet.

---

[4] Neihardt expressed this idea in an interview in the summer of 1957. As a young man he had associated intimately with the Omaha Indians, a Siouan people, on the reservation in Nebraska, and had made a study of their customs and language. In the thirties he developed a close friendship with the Oglala medicine man Black Elk, who trusted Neihardt enough to disclose his power vision and adopt the poet as his "spiritual son." Neihardt and his two oldest daughters were made members of the Oglala tribe in official ceremonies at Pine Ridge. In 1944 and 1945 Neihardt served under John Collier in the Office of Indian Affairs. His skill in picturing Indians sympathetically and in reproducing their idiom drew praise from the Indians themselves.

The Speech

WE ARE YOUNG NO LONGER (EASTMAN VERSION)

"Hay, hay, hay! Alas, alas!" Thus speaks the old man, when he knows that his former vigor and freedom is gone from him forever. So we may exclaim to-day, Alas! There is a time appointed to all things. Think for a moment how many multitudes of the animal tribes we ourselves have destroyed! Look upon the snow that appears to-day—to-morrow it is water! Listen to the dirge of the dry leaves, that were green and vigorous but a few moons before! We are a part of this life and it seems that our time is come.

Yet note how the decay of one nation invigorates another. This strange white man—consider him, his gifts are manifold! His tireless brain, his busy hand do wonders for his race. Those things which we despise he holds as treasures; yet he is so great and so flourishing that there must be some virtue and truth in his philosophy. I wish to say to you, my friends: Be not moved alone by heated arguments and thoughts of revenge! These are for the young. We are young no longer; let us think well, and give counsel as old men!

WE ARE YOUNG NO LONGER (NEIHARDT VERSION)

Hey—hey'-hey! So laments an aging man
Who totters and can never more be free
As once he was. Hey—hey'-hey! So may we
Exclaim today for what the morrow brings.
There is a time, my brothers, for all things,
And we are getting old. Consider, friends,
How everything begins and grows and ends
That other things may have their time and grow.
What tribes of deer and elk and buffalo
Have we ourselves destroyed lest we should die!
About us now you hear the dead leaves sigh;
Since these were green, how few the moons have been!

We share in all this trying to begin,
This trying not to die. Consider well
The White Man—what you know and what men tell
About his might. His never weary mind
And busy hands do magic for his kind.
Those things he loves we think of little worth;
And yet, behold! he sweeps across the earth,
And what shall stop him? Something that is true
Must help him do the things that he can do,
For lies are not so mighty. Be not stirred
By thoughts of vengeance and the burning word!
Such things are for the young; but let us give
Good counsel for the time we have to live,
And seek the better way, as old men should.

Further Reading

The indispensable book for a study of Spotted Tail is George E. Hyde's *Spotted Tail's Folk: A History of the Brulé Sioux* (Norman: University of Oklahoma Press, 1961), which restores perspective to the assessment of the Brulé chief's decisions and motives. For later events, Hyde's *A Sioux Chronicle* (Norman: University of Oklahoma Press, 1956) gives an excellent picture of the reservation years. Jacob P. Dunn's *Massacres of the Mountains: A History of the Indian Wars of the Far West 1815–1875* (New York: Archer House, Inc., n. d.) is not meticulously documented, but presents valuable source material, and Eastman's much condemned *Indian Heroes and Great Chieftains* (Boston: Little, Brown, and Co., 1918) is recognized even by its severe critics as a useful source. For background reading and various views of Spotted Tail and his influence, specially to be recommended are: Captain Eugene Ware, *The Indian War of 1864*, originally published in 1911, reissued with introduction and notes by Clyde C. Walter (New York: St. Martin's Press, 1960); George Bird Grinnell, *The Fighting Cheyennes* (Norman: University of Oklahoma Press, 1956); George E. Hyde, *Red Cloud's Folk* (Norman: University of Oklahoma Press, 1937); and Grace Hebard and E. A. Brininstool, *The Bozeman Trail* (Cleveland:

Arthur H. Clark Co., 1922; two vols.). One of the best of the recent studies is the thoroughly documented and readable *Red Cloud and the Sioux Problem* by James C. Olson, former director of the Nebraska State Historical Society (Lincoln: University of Nebraska Press, 1965).

CHAPTER **6**

Eulogy to the Dog

GEORGE GRAHAM VEST

*The people who are prone to fall on their knees
to do us honor when success is with us may be
the first to throw the stone of malice when failure
settles its cloud upon our heads.*

—GEORGE GRAHAM VEST

The Speaker

GEORGE GRAHAM VEST was born in Frankfort, Kentucky, on
December 6, 1830. A graduate of Centre College (1848) and
of Transylvania University (in law, 1853), he moved to Missouri in 1854 and in 1856 began the practice of law in Boon-
ville. Throughout his adult life he was active in the practice
of law and in politics. In 1860 he was a presidential elector
pledged to Stephen A. Douglas. In the same year, as an acknowledged supporter of the South, he was elected to the
Missouri House of Representatives; and at the rump session of
the Missouri legislature held at Neosho in 1861, he was chosen
as a Representative from Missouri to the Confederate Congress.
Later (1865) he was named Senator from Missouri to the
Confederacy, and still later (1879–1903) he served as United
States Senator from Missouri. Considered to be conservative,
even reactionary, he stated eloquently the views held by many

45

of his fellow-countrymen on the protective tariff (he opposed it) and on the acquisition of Puerto Rico and the Philippines (he thought it unconstitutional). A brilliant lawyer, Vest was greatly renowned as a pleader before juries. Ironically, his fame rests not upon the major questions on which he spoke—the Kellogg case, the attack on the McKinley Tariff, the nomination of "Silver Dick" Bland—but on an accomplishment of which he apparently took little note: his famous eulogy to the dog.

George Graham Vest died on August 9, 1904, at Sweet Springs, Missouri, and was buried in Bellefontaine Cemetery, St. Louis.

The text for Vest's "Eulogy to the Dog" is taken (with Mr. Kuhr's permission) from the University-Microfilms edition of Manuel I. Kuhr's doctoral dissertation, "The Speaking Career of George Graham Vest," submitted at the University of Missouri in 1963. Mr. Kuhr states (p. 85) that the text he provides is taken "from the earliest known publication of the speech in the Chicago *Herald,* September 17, 1897."

The Occasion

As an institution is said to be the lengthened shadow of a man, so a speech may be a foreshortened shadow of a man or of a culture. In an urban society a dog may become a mere adornment, a symbol of conspicuous consumption. To the American frontiersman and early settler, however, his dog was a member of the family—sometimes no less regarded than his children. Not unwittingly did George Caleb Bingham, the Missouri artist roughly contemporary with George Graham Vest, place two dogs in the foreground of his representation of Missourians listening to a stump speaker. Particularly to those Missourians, of whom there were many, whose forebears came from the South—North Carolina, Virginia, Kentucky, Tennessee —the dog was fellow-creature and friend, and above all, companion of the hunt. Only those who have followed a well-tuned hound baying across bottom lands in pursuit of a night-wandering raccoon or possum are prepared fully to understand a rural Missourian's devotion to his dog.

In the Missouri of 1870, the fears and hatreds of the Civil War—of which Missouri was one of the battlegrounds—had been succeeded by the feuds of reconstruction. Alienated from their fellow-men by nameless cruelties observed or suffered in the guerrilla tactics of the Civil War, and by fears engendered by outlaw bands still at large during the period of reconstruction, a jury of Missourians was well-prepared to accept the thesis that man's best friend is his dog. To such a jury George Graham Vest spoke when the case of Burden *vs.* Hornsby came to trial on Thursday, September 22, 1870, in the old courthouse in Warrensburg, Missouri.

Charles Burden and Leonidas Hornsby were brothers-in-law who lived on neighboring farms in Johnson County.[1] According to an entirely credible tradition, they had fought on opposite sides in the Civil War. Hornsby, a former Tennessean, was thirty-two years old in 1870. He kept a flock of sheep; he testified that more than 100 had been killed by marauding dogs. Burden, born in Kentucky, liked to hunt. He kept a pack of hounds, of which the best was Old Drum, reputed to be the fastest, keenest, most relentless hound known in a community where men were good judges of dogs. Old Drum's regular, musical, well-tuned baying could be relied on to guide his master in the hunt.

Burden last heard Old Drum on the evening of October 28, 1869. The next day, Burden found Old Drum's body, riddled with shot, at a ford in Big Creek. Concluding that Hornsby was responsible, Burden brought suit against him for $100. At a trial before a justice of the peace on January 27, the jury found for the plaintiff and assessed Hornsby $25 and costs. Hornsby retained Crittenden and Cockrell, among the most eminent attorneys in Missouri, and appealed to the Johnson County Court of Common Pleas. Burden retained Elliott and Blodgett. The case was heard in the March term, and Judge A. R. Conklin, sitting without a jury, found for Hornsby. Burden's attorneys filed a motion for a new trial and the motion was sustained; the trial was set for the September term, almost a year after Old Drum's body had been found.

According to tradition, Vest, who was in attendance on other business, entered the case at the request of Wells Blodgett,

[1] The account that follows relies chiefly on "The Speaking Career of George Graham Vest," by Dr. Manuel I. Kuhr, to whom the editors express their indebtedness.

one of Burden's attorneys, after the trial was under way. After hearing extensive testimony, the judge allowed each side four hours for speeches summing up the case. Colonel Blodgett opened for the plaintiff and was followed by attorneys Crittenden and Cockrell for Hornsby. The Court then stood in recess until the following morning, when, according to Crittenden, who was the opposing counsel, Vest delivered "as perfect and grand a piece of oratory as was ever heard from pulpit or bar." Of Vest's speech only the closing portion, known as the "Eulogy to the Dog" has been preserved.

Following Vest's speech, the jury at once returned a verdict for Burden, with damages of $500, of which the excess beyond Burden's claim of $50 was remitted. Hornsby appealed to the Supreme Court of Missouri, which, in July, 1872, handed down a verdict for Burden. In 1958, the city of Warrensburg, Missouri, erected to Drum a monument inscribed with the language of George Graham Vest's "Eulogy to the Dog."

The Speech

EULOGY TO THE DOG

GENTLEMEN OF THE JURY: *The best friend a man has in this world may turn against him and become his enemy. His son or daughter that he has reared with loving care may prove ungrateful. Those who are nearest and dearest to us, those whom we trust with our happiness and our good name, may become traitors to their faith. The money that a man has he may lose. It flies away from him, perhaps when he needs it most. A man's reputation may be sacrificed in a moment of ill-considered action. The people who are prone to fall on their knees to do us honor when success is with us may be the first to throw the stone of malice when failure settles its cloud upon our heads. The one absolutely unselfish friend that man can have in this selfish world, the one that never deserts him, the one that never proves ungrateful or treacherous, is his dog.*

Gentlemen of the jury, a man's dog stands by him in prosperity and poverty, in health and sickness. He will sleep on the cold ground, where the wintry winds blow and the snow drives fiercely, if only he may be near his master's side. He will kiss the hand that has no food to offer, he will lick the wounds and sores that come in encounter with the roughness of the world. He guards the sleep of his pauper master as if he were a prince. When all other friends desert he remains. When riches take wings and reputation falls to pieces he is as constant in his love as the sun in its journey through the heavens. If fortune drives the master forth an outcast in the world, friendless and homeless, the faithful dog asks no higher privilege than of accompanying him to guard against danger, to fight against his enemies. And when the last scene of all comes, and death takes the master in its embrace and his body is laid away in the cold ground, no matter if all other friends pursue their way, there by his graveside will the noble dog be found, his head between his paws, his eyes sad but open in alert watchfulness, faithful and true even in death.

Further Reading

Those interested in reading further concerning Senator George Graham Vest and his "Eulogy to the Dog" must go to sources not conveniently published. The best bibliography, that supplied by Manuel I. Kuhr in his doctoral dissertation, "The Speaking Career of George Graham Vest," lists letters, newspaper and magazine articles, court records, and other documents, as well as books in which Vest is mentioned; but it lists no biographies, critical or otherwise. A short sketch in the *Dictionary of American Biography* provides only essential facts about Vest. Apparently the only book now in print solely concerning him is one by F. M. C. French, *Senator Vest: Champion of the Dog* (Boston: Meador Publishing Co., 1930).

CHAPTER 7

Address for the Unknown
Loyal Dead

FREDERICK DOUGLASS

*Dark and sad will be the hour to this nation
when it forgets to pay grateful homage to its greatest benefactors.*

—FREDERICK DOUGLASS

The Speaker

FREDERICK DOUGLASS, one of the most remarkable men to
come out of American slavery, was born *nullius filius* in Talbot
County, on the Eastern shore of Maryland, probably in February, 1817, of a slave mother (Harriet Bailey) and of father unknown. Of birth into slavery, Douglass observed in his *Life and
Times* (p. 27), "Slavery had no recognition of fathers, as none
of families. . . . The father might be a white man, glorying in
the purity of his Anglo-Saxon blood, and his child ranked with
the blackest slaves." On escaping from slavery in 1838, he chose
"Frederick Douglass" as the name by which he was known
thereafter. Douglass was a powerful orator of gifted phrase
who moved men and women actively to oppose slavery. After
the Civil War he continued in public life to support civil rights
for Negroes, and he served as Marshal of the District of Columbia (1877–1881), as well as in other offices. He died in
1895.

The text for "Address for the Unknown Loyal Dead" is to be found in Frederick Douglass, *Life and Times of Frederick Douglass* . . . (Hartford, Conn.: Park Publishing Co., 1882), pp. 461–63. Presumably the text was supplied by Douglass himself.

The Occasion

On November 19, 1863, Abraham Lincoln, President of the United States, delivered at Gettysburg the speech that has become a part of the American legend. Less than eight years later, on Decoration Day, 1871, Frederick Douglass, once a fugitive slave ransomed by the charity of British subjects, delivered at Arlington a comparable address, but less well known, dedicating a monument to "Unknown Loyal Dead."

Comparisons and contrasts between the orators, as well as the occasions, are easy to discover. Both Douglass and Lincoln had risen in station, the one from slavery, the other from poverty and obscurity. Both men had gained the respect of many of their fellow countrymen and the hatred of others. Both men had learned in the school of experience how to use language effectively to express both reason and passion. Both men had triumphed over adversity, but the triumph of Frederick Douglass —born a nameless slave without any rights his masters were bound to respect—was even more spectacular than that of Abraham Lincoln. For Douglass had not only to escape from poverty and obscurity, as did Lincoln. He had also to escape from the lowest condition in which man can find himself: a state in which, without real protection from the laws, his body and indeed to a degree his mind and spirit belong to someone else. But Douglass employed courage, intelligence, ingenuity, and some good fortune to escape from slavery. There is in American biography no more moving story than the account of Frederick Douglass' adversity and his triumph over it: the slave quarters into which he was born, his mother's devotion and early death, the kindness of some "white folks" and the unrestrained cruelty of others, his learning to read and the firing of his imagination, his attempts to escape, his fights with white apprentices, his sufferings from the overseers, his escape from Maryland to Massachusetts, his marriage, his travel to England, his discovery that in some quarters black men can be respected for what they are, his purchase and manumission by English friends, his return to his own country, his founding of a newspaper, his support of the "underground railroad," his quarrels with William Lloyd Garrison, his meeting with John Brown of Osawatomie, his recruiting of colored regiments in the Civil War, the honors given him after the War, and, not the least of his experiences, his successes in public speaking.

Douglass' reputation as an orator justified his being chosen to deliver the dedicatory address at Arlington. Well known as a public figure, he was in 1871 at the height of those powers first manifested in the remarkable speech delivered at a meeting of the Anti-Slavery Society in Nantucket, Massachusetts, in the summer of 1841. Following this impromptu speech that revealed from bitter personal experience the horrors that could exist under slavery, Douglass had immediately been enlisted as an agent of the Massachusetts Anti-Slavery Society, thus to begin a career in speechmaking that lasted throughout his life. For thirty years prior to 1871 he had thus perfected himself in the knowledge of audiences and the art of speechmaking.

Frederick Douglass' address at Arlington was delivered in impressive circumstances. Among those present were President Ulysses S. Grant and the members of his cabinet, with other distinguished citizens assembled to do honor to the unknown soldiers who had died in the service of the United States during the Civil War. In his address Douglass endeavored to express "the true view which should be taken of the great conflict between slavery and freedom." [1]

The Speech

ADDRESS FOR THE UNKNOWN LOYAL DEAD

FRIENDS AND FELLOW CITIZENS: *Tarry here for a moment. My words shall be few and simple. The solemn rites of this hour and place call for no lengthened speech. There is in the very air of this resting ground of the unknown dead a silent, subtle, and an all-pervading eloquence, far more touching, im-*

[1] Douglass, *op. cit.,* p. 461.

*pressive, and thrilling than living lips have ever uttered. Into
the measureless depths of every loyal soul it is now whispering
lessons of all that is precious, priceless, holiest, and most enduring in human existence.*

*Dark and sad will be the hour to this nation when it forgets
to pay grateful homage to its greatest benefactors. The offering we bring to-day is due alike to the patriot soldiers dead and
their noble comrades who still live; for whether living or dead,
whether in time or eternity, the loyal soldiers who imperiled
all for country and freedom are one and inseparable.*

*Those unknown heroes whose whitened bones have been pi-
ously gathered here, and whose green graves we now strew
with sweet and beautiful flowers, choice emblems alike of pure
hearts and brave spirits, reached in their glorious career that
last highest point of nobleness beyond which human power
cannot go. They died for their country.*

*No loftier tribute can be paid to the most illustrious of all
the benefactors of mankind than we pay to these unrecognized
soldiers, when we write above their graves this shining epitaph.*

*When the dark and vengeful spirit of slavery, always ambi-
tious, preferring to rule in hell than to serve in heaven, fired the
Southern heart and stirred all the malign elements of discord;
when our great Republic, the hope of freedom and self-government throughout the world, had reached the point of supreme
peril; when the Union of those States was torn and rent asunder
at the center, and the armies of a gigantic rebellion came forth
with broad blades and bloody hands to destroy the very foun-
dation of American society, the unknown braves who flung
themselves into the yawning chasm, where cannon roared and
bullets whistled, fought and fell. They died for their country.*

*We are sometimes asked, in the name of patriotism, to for-
get the merits of this fearful struggle, and to remember with
equal admiration those who struck at the nation's life and those
who struck to save it,—those who fought for slavery and those
who fought for liberty and justice.*

*I am no minister of malice. I would not strike the fallen. I
would not repel the repentant, but may my "right hand forget
her cunning, and my tongue cleave to the roof of my mouth,"
if I forget the difference between the parties to that terrible,
protracted, and bloody conflict.*

If we ought to forget a war which has filled our land with widows and orphans, which has made stumps of men of the very flower of our youth; sent them on the journey of life armless, legless, maimed and mutilated; which has piled up a debt heavier than a mountain of gold—swept uncounted thousands of men into bloody graves, and planted agony at a million hearthstones; I say if this war is to be forgotten, I ask in the name of all things sacred what shall men remember?

The essence and significance of our devotions here to-day are not to be found in the fact that the men whose remains fill these graves were brave in battle. If we met simply to show our sense of bravery, we should find enough to kindle admiration on both sides. In the raging storm of fire and blood, in the fierce torrent of shot and shell, of sword and bayonet, whether on foot or on horse, unflinching courage marked the rebel not less than the loyal soldier.

But we are not here to applaud manly courage, save as it has been displayed in a noble cause. We must never forget that victory to the rebellion meant death to the republic. We must never forget that the loyal soldiers who rest beneath this sod flung themselves between the nation and the nation's destroyers. If to-day we have a country not boiling in an agony of blood like France; if now we have a united country, no longer cursed by the hell-black system of human bondage; if the American name is no longer a by-word and a hissing to a mocking earth; if the star spangled banner floats only over free American citizens in every quarter of the land, and our country has before it a long and glorious career of justice, liberty, and civilization, we are indebted to the unselfish devotion of the noble army who rest in these honored graves all around us."

Further Reading

The *Life and Times of Frederick Douglass . . .* (Hartford, Conn.: Park Publishing Co., 1882) is Douglass' own story of his life—and the best one (a revision was published in 1941). It covers the materials first published (1845) in *Narrative of the Life of Frederick Douglass* and recently (1960) reissued by the Harvard University Press with an introduction by Benjamin

Quarles, who is also the author of *Frederick Douglass* (Washington, D. C.: The Associated Publishers, Inc., 1948). Of special interest is the biography by Booker T. Washington, *Frederick Douglass* (Philadelphia: George W. Jacobs & Co., 1906). Two somewhat fictionalized biographies make easy reading: Shirley Graham's *There Was Once a Slave: The Heroic Story of Frederick Douglass* (New York: Julian Messner, Inc., 1947), and Edmund Fuller's *A Star Pointed North* (New York: Harper & Brothers, 1946).

CHAPTER 8

His Majesty's Address to the People of Lahaina

KING DAVID KALAKAUA

Figures of the census have been published to show that we are a dying race. But shall we sit still, and indolently see the structure created by our fathers fall to pieces without lifting a hand to stay the work of destruction?

—KING DAVID KALAKAUA

The Speaker

DAVID KALAKAUA, the last King of Hawaii, was born in Honolulu on November 16, 1836. On February 12, 1874, over the strong objection of the Dowager Queen Emma, the legislature chose him king to succeed Lunalilo. The rioting that followed his election was put down by troops landed from British and American warships, and order was restored. With this inauspicious beginning, Kalakaua began an eventful reign. In 1874 he visited the United States, where he was accorded all the honors due royalty. In 1875 a treaty of reciprocity (renewed in 1887) was negotiated between Hawaii and the United States. In 1881 Kalakaua made a world tour. In 1887 he yielded to demands for a new constitution, which was duly ratified by popular vote. During Kalakaua's reign attention was given to problems of immigration. Arrangements were made for bringing in Portu-

57

guese families from the Azores, Polynesians from the Gilbert Islands, and workers from Japan. Immigration from Hong Kong was discouraged. Kalakaua died on January 20, 1891, in San Francisco where he had gone for medical attention, and was succeeded by Queen Liliuokalani.

Kalakaua endeavored to rule personally. Inasmuch as his reign occurred during a time of unparalleled prosperity in Hawaii, his extravagances were less deplored than they might have been otherwise; and he is remembered for his good humor rather than for his lapses. His genial manners and easy-going disposition caused him to be known as "the merry monarch."

"His Majesty's Address to the People of Lahaina" is translated from the Hawaiian as it appeared in the *Pacific Commercial Advertiser* of April 18, 1874.[1]

The Occasion

In 1874, when King William C. Lunalilo died without an heir and without having designated a successor, he left his kingdom with a special problem of the succession; for Lunalilo's death ended a dynasty as well as a reign. He was the last of the blood line of the Kamehamehas. The choice of a new ruler fell to the Legislature. There were two candidates: the Dowager Queen, Emma, and Kalakaua, descendant of Chiefs high among the *alii,* or aristocracy. In spite of her handicap of femininity, Emma was the popular choice of the native Hawaiians. Kalakaua, who had declared his candidacy on the day following the death of Lunalilo, was—for good reasons or bad—the choice of the Legislature and of those leaders of opinion, particularly among the Americans, who feared that Queen Emma, a friend and admirer of the British Queen Victoria, might not be sympathetic to the United States. When, on February 12, 1874, the Legislature by a vote of 39 to 6 elected Kalakaua, a mob attacked the members of the Legis-

---

[1] The statement concerning King Kalakaua and "His Majesty's Address to the People of Lahaina" is based on a newspaper account contemporary with the speech, on the works listed in the section on further reading, and on conversations in Hawaii, notably with some of the *alii* and with Elizabeth Kunimoto, Instructor in Speech, the University of Hawaii, whose master's thesis is a contribution to the literature of oratory in Hawaii.

lature. In the ensuing violence the legislative chambers were sacked and official documents destroyed, a number of persons were injured, and one man was killed. The disturbance was quieted on the following day when, on Kalakaua's taking the royal oath, Emma recognized him as Sovereign. Nevertheless, Kalakaua was doubtless well-advised to conduct a royal progress throughout the islands that constituted his kingdom and to employ his personal charms, which were many, to the prosperity of his throne.

Kalakaua's speech at Lahaina was thus designed to announce his policies, to win favor with his people, and to consolidate his position as ruler. Lahaina, a capital city before Honolulu became the center of the Hawaiian kingdom, was the obvious site on the island of Maui for the speech to be delivered in the course of the royal progress. Whether Kalakaua wrote "His Majesty's Address to the People of Lahaina" as it was delivered on April 13, 1874, or—like many another monarch had it prepared for him by his ministers—is not known. However, it is clear that King Kalakaua was quite capable of inditing an address. Kalakaua was in 1874, and increasingly thereafter, not only a royal personage but a gentleman of rare charm and of some sophistication in social if not in high political matters. As an editor, an author, a composer (of the national anthem, "Hawaii Ponoi"), a patron of the arts, and a *bon vivant,* he could have held his own with the kings of all Christendom. He could not only consort with kings, but be one—nor lose the common touch.

As an orator, Kalakaua, if he applied himself to the task, would have found as little difficulty in writing a speech as in delivering it. "His Majesty's Address to the People of Lahaina" demonstrates a facility in the arts of oral discourse in which Kalakaua's forebears, without a written language, had achieved a high degree of mastery. Sir Peter Buck has written learnedly of the Polynesian uses of oratory, to which Kalakaua fell heir along with his race and his kingship:

The occasions for oratory were numerous. All visitors from another tribe or district had to be welcomed officially with speeches, and they had to reply to their hosts. A member of a tribe who had been absent for some time was received back with welcoming speeches to which he replied. Owing to the social system which grouped people together into communities or tribes, the individual was regarded as representing his group. Thus no visitor could slip quietly into a village as an individual; etiquette demanded that he be welcomed officially by the chiefs of the community he visited. At feasts, marriages, and funerals, orations formed a necessary part of the procedure. In family and group discussions regarding economic matters such as food supplies, matters were formally thrashed out by the leaders delivering speeches. Other matters of public importance such as war were discussed in public either in the open village plaza or within the guest, or meeting, house. The chiefs and leaders spoke while the mass of the people formed their audience.[2]

The King's address demonstrates a sophistication in the arts of discourse that would do credit to any language. His gracious references to William C. Lunalilo, who was much beloved; his mention of his Queen, the lovely and gracious Kapiolani; his reminders of Kamehameha I and "the law of the broken paddle"; of Kamehameha II and the breaking of the tabu; of Kamehameha III and his promulgation of the law of righteousness —all of these preceding the enunciation of his own policy and his own admonition—gave authority to his utterance and established him in the Hawaiian royal tradition.

The Speech

HIS MAJESTY'S ADDRESS TO THE PEOPLE OF LAHAINA

PEOPLE OF LAHAINA: *Before addressing to you the brief remarks which I propose to make on this occasion, I cannot omit referring to some memories of my late lamented Predecessor, who made a short visit here last year, on the journey which he undertook for the benefit of his health. The late King was deeply solicitous for the welfare of his people, but the condition of his health was such that he was unable to carry out his plans for their good. I regarded the late King and his two immediate predecessors with strong affection, for on these sands and among these fields of Lahaina, they and I have played together as boys, in the family of our grandmother, Hoapili Wahine. The recollections of those days long past come before me vividly now.*

And now I have come hither to see you, as my children, and

2 Sir Peter H. Buck, "Polynesian Oratory," in *Ancient Hawaiian Civilization,* Chapter 16, p. 163.

that you may look upon me as your father. I thank you much, people of the district of Lahaina, for the very warm and loyal reception which you have given us, one which neither myself, the Queen nor the members of the Royal Family can cease to remember with pleasure.

The principal object which I have had in view in making this journey among my people, is that we may all be incited to renewed exertions for the advancement and prosperity of our nation, the extinction of which has been prophesied. Figures of the census have been published to show that we are a dying race. But shall we sit still, and indolently see the structure created by our fathers fall to pieces without lifting a hand to stay the work of destruction? If the house is dilapidated, let us repair it. Let us thoroughly renovate our own selves, to the end that causes of decay being removed, the nation may grow again with new life and vigor, and our Government may be firmly established—that structure which our fathers erected.

There are some of the old folks remaining and here present, the people of the time of Kamehameha I, who heard that celebrated saying: "The old men, the old women, and the children may sleep by the wayside without fear." That motto remains good to this day. Kamehameha II broke the tabu on social intercourse—his word was, O ka ainoa. Said Kamehameha III, "The righteous man is my man," and this sentiment prevails today among us, both foreigners and natives. I believe that if I shall make the main object of my reign the increase of the nation, there may be secured both the stability of the Government and the national independence. Then let my motto be—"The man and woman who shall live correctly and bring forth children, they are my people." And I charge you parents, take every care of your little ones. And to you children also I say, obey your parents.

The increase of the people, the advancement of agriculture and commerce:—these are the objects which my Government will mainly strive to accomplish.

Further Reading

The standard work concerning Hawaii is Ralph S. Kuykendall, *The Hawaiian Kingdom* (Honolulu: The University of Hawaii

Press, 1938 *et seq.*), 3 vols. In a narrative beginning with the discovery of the islands by Captain James Cook and concluding with the reign of Queen Liliuokalani, the volumes meet a high standard of historical scholarship. A shorter well-written account is A. Grove Day's *Hawaii and Its People* (New York: Duell, Sloan and Pearce, 1955). The chapter entitled "The Decline and Fall of the Monarchy" (pp. 199–218) is especially relevant to the reign of Kalakaua. *A Hawaiian Reader* (New York: Popular Library, 1959), edited by A. Grove Day and Carl Stroven, with an introduction by James Michener, provides an excellent selection of articles concerning the fiftieth state. Thomas Blake Clark, *Paradise Limited: An Informal History of the Fabulous Hawaiians* (New York: Modern Age Books, 1941) includes chapters concerning Kalakaua and life in Hawaii during his reign. Eugene Burns, *The Last King of Paradise* (New York: Pellegrini and Cudahy, 1952) is a somewhat sentimentalized biography of Kalakaua. William N. Armstrong, *Around the World with a King* (New York: Frederick A. Stokes Co., 1904) is a circumstantial account of King Kalakaua's world tour of 1881.

King Kalakaua was himself credited with *The Legends and Myths of Hawaii: The Fables and Folk-Lore of a Strange People*, as edited by R. M. Daggett (New York: Charles L. Webster & Co., 1888).

Hawaii has been the subject of a number of novels, of which two may be mentioned: James Michener, *Hawaii* (New York: Random House, 1959), and O. A. Bushnell, *The Return of Lono: A Novel of Captain Cook's Last Voyage* (Boston: Little, Brown and Co., 1956). Other volumes concerning Hawaii, but of less relevance to Kalakaua, are Stanley D. Porteus, *And Blow Not the Trumpet: A Prelude to Peril* (Palo Alto, California: Pacific Books, 1947); Francis John Halford, M.D., *9 Doctors and God* (Honolulu: University of Hawaii Press, 1954); and Joseph Barber Jr., *Hawaii: Restless Rampart* (Indianapolis: The Bobbs-Merrill Co., 1941).

Ancient Hawaiian Civilization, by Messrs. Handy, Emory, Buck, Wise, and others (Honolulu: The Kamehameha Schools, 1933) is a series of lectures.

CHAPTER 9

The Surrender Speech

CHIEF JOSEPH

*From where the sun now stands I will fight no
more forever.*

—CHIEF JOSEPH OF THE NEZ PERCE

The Speaker

CHIEF JOSEPH of the Nez Perce, known to his own people
as Hin-mah-too-yah-lat-kekht (Thunder Traveling to the Loftier
Mountain Heights), was probably born in 1840. He died in 1904.
After his surrender to the United States Army in 1877, he was
sent with his people to a reservation in the Indian Territory.
In 1885 he was transferred to the Colville reservation in Wash-
ington, but was never again permitted to settle in the beautiful
Wallowa country of Oregon that was his home.

The text of Chief Joseph's "Surrender Speech" is taken *verbatim* from *Harper's Weekly*, Vol. 21, No. 1090 (November 17,
1877), p. 906. Of this text, it was reported, "Our artist was
the only person present who committed the proceedings to writing, and took the reply as it came from the lips of the speaker."
Probably the artist was Lieutenant C. E. S. Wood, who presumably took down the speech as it was interpreted by Arthur
Chapman, a white man well known to the Nez Perce as well
as to General O. O. Howard and his soldiers.

Mark H. Brown, in *The Flight of the Nez Perce* (pp. 407–408) discredits the received account of the Nez Perce surrender. He does not refer to the article in *Harper's Weekly*.

The Occasion

Of the many conflicts between Indians and white men in North America, perhaps none shows the Indians to better advantage, and none is better documented, than the resistance of the Nez Perce in 1877. Invited, as they thought, to a council with General O. O. Howard, the chiefs of several Nez Perce bands were not offered treaties but were ordered to give up their homelands and move to a reservation in Idaho, where other Nez Perce were already living. Toohoolhoolzote, one of the most respected leaders, was detained in a stockade because of his outburst against the white man's authority. General Howard's orders eventually left little ground for argument: the Nez Perce could either go quietly or be taken by force from their tribal home in the Wallowa, one of the loveliest valleys in the world, to a new and strange reservation. Given thirty days to move all their belongings, their herds, and their families, the Nez Perce accepted the advice of their chiefs—the two brothers, Joseph and Ollokot—to accede to General Howard's demands rather than go to war.

Collecting such of their possessions as they could carry, and such of their cattle and horses as they could round up, Chief Joseph's band took a trail that led them across the Snake River, where they lost some of their possessions and many of their cattle, on to Tolo Lake,[1] where they found other bands already encamped.

As the Indians, particularly the young men, exchanged stories of indignities suffered and wrongs imposed, they became increasingly bitter. The elders, who recognized their helplessness in prolonged conflict with the white men, counseled patience and peace; but on June 12, 1877, some of the Indians, discountenancing their chiefs, put on a war parade. The next day, three young men of the Nez Perce, stirred by taunts of cowardice and by a sense of indignities suffered, left the camp on

---

[1] Tolo Lake is near what is now Grangeville, Idaho.

a mission to kill those white men whose previous conduct had given the Indians warrant to take vengeance.

Within a few days Indian warriors had killed or wounded a number of white settlers on the Salmon River and spread the fear of an Indian uprising throughout the countryside. Although the two warriors primarily responsible for the initial murders did not return to the camp at Tolo Lake, the youngest—Swan Necklace, a lad of seventeen—did return to tell the exciting story of the raid to men all too eager to hear it. Chiefs Joseph and Ollokot continued to plead for a policy of patience and peace, but the rising war spirit was too strong for them. Save for a few members of other bands and their own band from the Wallowa country, they were deserted by the Indians, of whom the young men took to the warpath and the old men, the women, and the children sought refuge in a remote canyon.

The further story of Chief Joseph and the Nez Perce is one of privation, fortitude, and leadership unsurpassed in the annals of the Indian wars. As the bands on the warpath attacked homesteads and travelers, troops of the United States cavalry were ordered out by General O. O. Howard, the while Chief Joseph and his band remained encamped debating what to do when the soldiers came. The headmen decided that, on the appearance of the soldiers, six men would offer a flag of truce; but the opportunity for a parley was lost when one of the volunteers with the troopers under command of Captain David Perry, either not seeing or ignoring the flag of truce, fired a shot. The Indians returned the fire. In the ensuing fierce battle of White Bird Canyon, the troopers were defeated and fled with the Indians in hot pursuit. Without the loss of a single man, the Indians killed a third of Captain Perry's force and— highly important to them—took both rifles and pistols from the battlefield. As the wise men know, however, the victory was disastrous: it encouraged the warriors in a conflict they could not hope to win and it required the soldiers of the United States to undertake a conflict they could not lose. Believing themselves to face another Indian war, the settlers demanded protection that was not long in coming. Troops were ordered out not only from the Northwest but from California, Arizona, and Georgia to suppress an uprising.

The Indian chiefs, aware that they must now expect the arrival of new troops of United States cavalry, pursued a plan of evasion and retreat comparable to the successful withdrawal to Canada undertaken by Sitting Bull a year earlier.

Not a leader of warriors, as was his brother Ollokot, nor a leader in Council, as was Toohoolhoolzote, Chief Joseph was honored with a responsibility considered sacred by his peers: the protection of the helpless—the old men, the women, and the children. As the summer wore on, and as Joseph's responsibility grew more and more grave, his stature increased. Among his own people, as among his enemies, he became the symbol both of sturdy resistance and of magnanimity, as manifested in his refraining from molesting white settlers. In the end, on October 5, 1877, after a retreat of 1,300 miles toward Canada, without food, with desolate mountain winter approaching, after successive battles, evasions, and retreats, the remaining Nez Perce found themselves—more children surviving than men, and more women than children—surrounded by overwhelming force. Finally, "after the longest and most successful march ever made by hostile Indians," [2] the Nez Perce permitted Chief Joseph to negotiate their surrender. Following the negotiations, Joseph came forward, with bullet holes in his clothing and bullet scratches on his body, to say the poignant words surrendering his people to the white soldiers. His speech, certainly one of the most famous ever spoken by an Indian chief, affected those who heard it at the time, as it has those who have read it since, with its cryptic sadness and forlorn beauty.

The Speech

THE SURRENDER SPEECH

Tell General Howard I know his heart. What he told me before, I have it in my heart. I am tired of fighting. Our chiefs are killed; Looking-Glass *is dead,* Ta-Hool-Hool-Shute *is dead. The old men are all dead. It is the young men who say "Yes" or*

---

[2] General Nelson A. Miles, *Serving the Republic* (New York: Harper & Brothers, 1911), p. 173.

"No." He who led on the young men is dead.[3] *It is cold, and we have no blankets; the little children are freezing to death. My people, some of them, have run away to the hills, and have no blankets, no food. No one knows where they are—perhaps freezing to death. I want to have time to look for my children, and see how many of them I can find. Maybe I shall find them among the dead. Hear me, my chiefs! I am tired; my heart is sick and sad. From where the sun now stands I will fight no more forever.*

Further Reading

The fate of the Nez Perce Indians has not ceased to attract the interest of anthropologists, historians, and scholars generally. In particular, Chief Joseph, who has come to be the symbol of the stout-hearted resistance offered by the Nez Perce against overwhelming odds, has been the subject of legend, story, and biography. The manuscript and printed material for the study of Chief Joseph and his band is now so considerable as to intimidate the casual reader. One indispensable book is the work by Alvin M. Josephy, Jr., *The Nez Perce Indians and the Opening of the Northwest* (New Haven: Yale University Press, 1965). Although the author modestly describes his book as "written primarily for the general reader" it is an object lesson in the uses of scholarship. The bibliography (pages 677–90) will provide ample suggestions for those whose interest is roused by the book itself. For a short account of Chief Joseph's resistance and surrender, one may read Mr. Josephy's article, "The Last Stand of Chief Joseph," in *American Heritage*, Vol. IX, No. 2 (February, 1958), pp. 36–43, 78–81. Both the book and the article are illuminated by excellent sketches and illustrations.

In *"I Will Fight No More Forever": Chief Joseph and the Nez Perce War* (Seattle: University of Washington Press, 1963) Merrill D. Beal gives an authoritative narrative of the Nez Perce War. In Chapter 22 (pp. 225–36) Beal describes the surrender of Chief Joseph and provides a text of his speech. In

---

[3] Perhaps Chief Joseph could not bear to speak the name of Ollokot, his much beloved brother.

his preface (p. xi) Beal offers a scholar's concurrence in the judgment of Secretary Carl Schurz: "This bloody conflict might have been avoided by a more careful regard for the rights of an Indian tribe whose former conduct had been uniformly peaceable and friendly."

Francis Haines' *The Nez Percés: Tribesmen of the Columbia Plateau* (Norman: The University of Oklahoma Press, 1955) is a scholarly account in which the author succeeds admirably in his attempt announced (p. ix) to treat the Nez Perce "primarily as human beings and to avoid, as far as possible, the stereotypes of Indians prevalent in some works."

Among the many other works likely to interest anyone wishing to know more about Chief Joseph and his speechmaking, as well as that of other Indian leaders, the following works may be suggested: Herbert Joseph Spinden, *The Nez Percé Indians,* in *Memoirs of the American Anthropological Association,* Vol. II (1907–1915); General O. O. Howard, *Nez Perce Joseph* (Boston: Lee and Shepard, Publishers, 1881); Chester Anders Fee, *Chief Joseph: The Biography of a Great Indian* (New York: Wilson-Erickson, Inc., 1936); Cyrus Townsend Brady, *Northwestern Fights and Fighters* (Garden City, New York: Doubleday, Page & Co., 1913); Virginia Weisel Johnson, *The Unregimented General: A Biography of Nelson A. Miles* (Boston: Houghton Mifflin Co., 1962); L. V. McWhorter, *Hear Me, My Chiefs: Nez Perce History and Legend* (Caldwell, Idaho: The Caxton Printers, Ltd., 1952); and, also by McWhorter, *Yellow Wolf: His Own Story* (Caldwell, Idaho: The Caxton Printers, Ltd., 1948).

Lt. Col. Mark H. Brown has explored unpublished sources in writing *The Flight of the Nez Perce* (New York, G. P. Putnam's Sons, 1967).

CHAPTER 10

A Tribute to
Ebon C. Ingersoll

ROBERT G. INGERSOLL

*The record of a generous life runs like a vine
around the memory of our dead, and every sweet,
unselfish act is now a perfumed flower.*

——ROBERT G. INGERSOLL

The Speaker

ROBERT GREEN INGERSOLL was born in Dresden, New York,
on August 11, 1833. He was the son of the Reverend John Ingersoll, a Congregational minister, and of Mary Livingston Ingersoll.
The Reverend John Ingersoll held many pastorates, in New York,
Ohio, Wisconsin, and finally in Illinois, where in 1854 Robert G.
Ingersoll was admitted to the Bar. Thereafter he achieved a
notable reputation as a jury pleader, and the law as vocation,
with politics and agnosticism as avocations, occupied him fully.
During the Civil War he organized a regiment of cavalry, of
which he was colonel, and saw service at Shiloh and Corinth.
Captured and paroled, he resigned his commission. Although he
had been a Democrat, he became a Republican and served as
Attorney-General of the state of Illinois (1867–69).

He was prominent in party politics, but his unpopular and
outspoken heterodoxy doubtless made him seem unavailable to
the party leaders. However, he did achieve a great reputation

in 1876 with his speech nominating James G. Blaine for the presidency. Ingersoll was best known in his own lifetime, and even today, as the champion of free thought and as the opponent of institutional religion. His knowledge of the Bible and of Christian doctrines and practices, together with his abilities as a speaker, enabled him to confound his opponents and to establish his views to the satisfaction of many of his fellow-countrymen. His influence was all the more effective because his personal conduct and family life were exemplary. Ingersoll died on July 21, 1899, following a heart attack, and is buried in Arlington Cemetery, Washington, D. C.

The text of Robert G. Ingersoll's "A Tribute to Ebon C. Ingersoll" is taken from *The Works of Robert G. Ingersoll* (New York: The Dresden Publishing Co., 1902), Vol. XII, pp. 389–91.

The Occasion

As an orator, Colonel Robert G. Ingersoll was mellifluous rather than profound.[1] He mastered and popularized a few rather simple concepts that made him anathema to the pietists of his day and brought him acclaim from those Americans who were breaking away from orthodoxy. His secret—perhaps the major one—was his mastery of an easy, felicitous, almost colloquial style both in phrasing and in presentation, a style peculiarly suitable to his generous spirit and warm personality. Hamlin Garland described Ingersoll's inimitable way of dealing with an audience:

He came on the vast stage alone, as I recall the scene, a large man in evening dress, quite bald and smoothly shaven. He began to speak almost before he left the wings, addressing himself to us with colloquial, unaffected directness. I say "to us," for that was precisely the effect he produced. He appeared to be speaking to each one of us individually. His tone was confidential, friendly, and yet authoritative. "Do you know," he began, "that every race has created all its gods and

[1] The statement concerning Robert G. Ingersoll and his speechmaking is based on contemporary newspaper accounts, on the works cited in the section on further reading, and on interviews with persons who heard him speak.

all its devils? The childhood of the race put fairies in the breeze and a kobold in the stream. Every religion began in exactly the same way."

These were not his exact words, of course, but such was the manner of his beginning. The stage was bare and he had no manuscript. Standing with his hands clasped behind his back, and speaking without effort, he made his words clear to every auditor. I was not especially concerned with his religious antagonism, but I enjoyed the beauty of his phrasing and the almost unequaled magic of his voice. He was a master of colloquial speech. Unlike Lowell, he eyed us, and laughed at us and with us. He bantered us, challenged us, electrified us. At times his eloquence held us silent as images and then some witty turn, some humorous phrase, brought roars of applause. At times we cheered almost every sentence like delegates at a political convention. At other moments we rose in our seats and yelled. There was something hypnotic in his rhythm as well as in his marvelous lines like a Saxon minstrel. His power over his auditors was absolute. His voice had no melody such as that of Booth possessed, but he had the singular power of making me oblivious of its quality. In the march of his ideas, in the pictures he drew, I forgot his bald head and his husky voice. As he spoke, all barriers between his mind and mine vanished. His effect on his hearers was magical, but the magic lay in his choice of words, rather than in beautiful enunciation.

As I studied him I came to the conclusion that a large part of his power lay in the fact that he vitalized every word, every syllable. He thought each sentence out at the moment he gave it utterance. He was alive to the tip of his tongue. He did not permit his organs of speech to proceed mechanically. He remained in control. . . .

He taught me the value of speaking as if thinking out loud. After hearing him, the harsh, monotonous cadences of other orators became a weariness [2]

Late in the afternoon of June 2, 1879, Robert G. Ingersoll had to employ his great talents in speechmaking to veil what he called "the deepest tragedy of my life." [3] The sudden death of his beloved brother required him, an agnostic, to offer what was, in effect, a funeral sermon. Indeed, Henry Ward Beecher, who read the funeral speech to his congregation at Plymouth Church,

[2] Hamlin Garland, *Roadside Meetings* (New York, 1930), p. 44, as quoted in W. Norwood Brigance, *A History and Criticism of American Public Address, Vol. I*, pp. 368–369.

[3] Orvin Larson, *American Infidel: Robert G. Ingersoll: A Biography*, p. 141.

Brooklyn, called it "one of the most exquisite yet one of the most
sad and mournful sermons that I ever read." [4]

The funeral occasion aroused great public interest, not only
because of the prominence of Ebon and Robert Ingersoll and
the celebrities who attended the funeral, but also because of
the unusual circumstance that no clergyman was to officiate.
The *National Republican* described the occasion:

The funeral of the Hon. E. C. Ingersoll took place yesterday afternoon at four o'clock, from his late residence, 1403 K Street. The
spacious parlors were filled to overflowing, and hundreds were unable
to obtain admittance. Among those who were present to pay their
homage to the distinguished and beloved dead were Secretary of the
Treasury Sherman, Assistant-Secretary of the Treasury Hawley, Sen-
ators Blaine, Voorhees, Paddock, David Davis, John A. Logan, the
Hon. William M. Morrison, Hon. William M. Springer, Hon. Thomas
A. Boyd, Governor Pound, Hon. J. R. Thomas, Hon. Thomas J.
Henderson, Hon. Jeremiah Wilson, Hon. Adlai E. Stevenson, Col.
Ward H. Lamon, Col. James Fishback, General Farnsworth, General
Robert C. Schenck, General Jeffries, General Williams and the Hon.
H. C. Burchard. Judge Shellabarger, General Birney, Governor Lowe,
Acting Commissioner of Internal Revenue H. C. Rogers, General
Williamson of the Land Office and a great many other prominent
members of the bar and also a large number of Illinoisans were pres-
ent. It was the largest gathering of distinguished persons assembled at
a funeral since that of Chief-Justice Chase.

The only ceremony at the house, other than the viewing of the remains, was a most affecting, pathetic, and touching address by Col.
Robert G. Ingersoll, brother of the deceased. Not only the speaker,
but every one of his hearers were deeply affected. When he began to
read his eloquent characterization of the dead man his eyes at once
filled with tears. He tried to hide them, but he could not do it, and
finally he bowed his head upon the dead man's coffin in uncontrollable
grief. It was only after some delay, and the greatest efforts at self-
mastery, that Colonel Ingersoll was able to finish reading his address.
When he had ceased speaking, the members of the bereaved family
approached the casket and looked upon the form which it contained,
for the last time. The scene was heartrending. The devotion of all
connected with the household excited the sympathy of all and there
was not a dry eye to be seen. The pall-bearers—Senator William B.
Allison, Senator James G. Blaine, Senator David Davis, Senator Daniel
W. Voorhees, Representative James A. Garfield, Senator A. S. Paddock,

[4] *Ibid.*, p. 143.

Representative Thomas Q. Boyd of Illinois, the Hon. Ward H. Lamon, ex-Congressman Jere Wilson, and Representative Adlai E. Stevenson of Illinois—then bore the remains to the hearse, and the lengthy cortege proceeded to the Oak Hill Cemetery, where the remains were interred, in the presence of the family and friends, without further ceremony.[5]

Some twenty years later the words Robert G. Ingersoll had said for his brother Ebon served again. At the funeral of Colonel Robert Green Ingersoll, in Dobbs Ferry, New York, on July 25, 1899, Dr. John Lovejoy Elliott read for the family and friends "A Tribute to Ebon C. Ingersoll." Some of the mourners heard for the second time, in similar circumstances, the felicitous but comfortless phrases:

Life is a narrow vale between the cold and barren peaks of two eternities. We strive in vain to look beyond the heights. We cry aloud, and the only answer is the echo to our wailing cry. From the voiceless lips of the unreplying dead there comes no word; but in the night of death—hope sees a star and listening love can hear the rustle of a wing.[6]

The Speech

A TRIBUTE TO EBON C. INGERSOLL

DEAR FRIENDS: *I am going to do that which the dead oft promised he would do for me.*

The loved and loving brother, husband, father, friend, died where manhood's morning almost touches noon, and while the shadows still were falling toward the west.

He had not passed on life's highway the stone that marks the highest point; but being weary for a moment, he lay down by the wayside, and using his burden for a pillow, fell into that dreamless sleep that kisses down his eyelids still. While yet in love with life and raptured with the world, he passed to silence and pathetic dust.

[5] *National Republican*, Washington, D. C., June 3, 1879, as quoted in *The Works of Robert G. Ingersoll* (New York: The Dresden Publishing Co., 1902), Vol. XII, p. 389.

[6] C. H. Cramer, *Royal Bob: The Life of Robert G. Ingersoll*, p. 263.

*Yet, after all, it may be best, just in the happiest, sunniest hour
of all the voyage, while eager winds are kissing every sail, to dash
against the unseen rock, and in an instant hear the billows roar
above a sunken ship. For whether in mid-sea or 'mong the break-
ers of the farther shore, a wreck at last must mark the end of
each and all. And every life, no matter if its every hour is rich
with love and every moment jeweled with a joy, will, at its close,
become a tragedy as sad and deep and dark as can be woven of
the warp and woof of mystery and death.*

*This brave and tender man in every storm of life was oak and
rock; but in the sunshine he was vine and flower. He was the
friend of all heroic souls. He climbed the heights, and left all
superstitions far below, while on his forehead fell the golden
dawning of the grander day.*

*He loved the beautiful, and was with color, form, and music
touched to tears. He sided with the weak, the poor, and wronged,
and lovingly gave alms. With loyal heart and with the purest
hands he faithfully discharged all public trusts.*

*He was a worshiper of liberty, a friend of the oppressed. A
thousand times I have heard him quote these words:* "For Justice
all place a temple, and all season, summer." *He believed that
happiness is the only good, reason the only torch, justice the only
worship, humanity the only religion, and love the only priest. He
added to the sum of human joy; and were every one to whom
he did some loving service to bring a blossom to his grave, he
would sleep tonight beneath a wilderness of flowers.*

*Life is a narrow vale between the cold and barren peaks of
two eternities. We strive in vain to look beyond the heights. We
cry aloud, and the only answer is the echo of our wailing cry.
From the voiceless lips of the unreplying dead there comes no
word; but in the night of death hope sees a star and listening
love can hear the rustle of a wing.*

*He who sleeps here, when dying, mistaking the approach of
death for the return of health, whispered with his latest breath,*
"I am better now." *Let us believe, in spite of doubts and dogmas,
of fears and tears, that these dear words are true of all the countless dead.*

*The record of a generous life runs like a vine around the mem-
ory of our dead, and every sweet, unselfish act is now a perfumed
flower.*

And now, to you, who have been chosen, from among the many men he loved, to do the last sad office for the dead, we give his sacred dust.

Speech cannot contain our love. There was, there is, no gentler, stronger, manlier man.

Further Reading

The speeches and lectures of Robert G. Ingersoll have been published in many editions and in many forms. *The Complete Works of Robert G. Ingersoll* (New York: The Ingersoll League, 1933), 12 vols., contains his major popular addresses. His granddaughter, Eva Ingersoll Wakefield, has edited *The Letters of Robert G. Ingersoll* (New York: Philosophical Library, 1951). *Ingersollia* . . . (Chicago: M. A. Donohue & Co., 1899), edited by Thomas W. Handford, is fairly typical of the many published volumes of excerpts from Ingersoll's speeches and lectures. A similar volume is Vera Goldthwaite's *The Philosophy of Ingersoll* (San Francisco: Paul Elder and Co., 1906). Chapman Cohen's *Bradlaugh and Ingersoll: A Centenary Appreciation of Two Great Reformers* (London: Pioneer Press, 1933) provides a perceptive comparison and contrast between the Englishman and the American. I. Newton Baker has edited *An Intimate View of Robert G. Ingersoll* (New York: C. P. Farrell, 1920), composed largely of tributes. Many books and tracts attacking Ingersoll and his views appeared during his lifetime. A representative work of this type is L. A. Lambert's *Notes on Ingersoll* (Buffalo, New York: Buffalo Catholic Publication Co., 1883).

Two biographies may be recommended: C. H. Cramer, *Royal Bob: The Life of Robert G. Ingersoll* (Indianapolis: The Bobbs-Merrill Co., Inc., 1952); and Orvin Larson, *American Infidel: Robert G. Ingersoll: A Biography* (New York: The Citadel Press, 1962). Larson's book, informed and sympathetic but not sentimental, is written in the perspective of the present day. A critical estimate of Ingersoll's speechmaking is provided in "Robert G. Ingersoll," by Wayland Maxfield Parrish and Alfred Dwight Huston, in W. Norwood Brigance (ed.), *A History and Criticism of American Public Address* (New York: McGraw-Hill Book Co., Inc., 1943), Vol. I, pp. 363–86.

CHAPTER 11

Responding to the New Call of Duty

WOODROW WILSON

Therefore, I congratulate you that you are going to live your lives under the most stimulating compulsion that any man can feel, the sense, not of private duty merely, but of public duty also.

—WOODROW WILSON

The Speaker

WOODROW WILSON, twenty-seventh President of the United States, was born at Staunton, Virginia, on December 28, 1856, the son of the Rev. Joseph Ruggles Wilson, a Presbyterian minister, and of Jessie Woodrow Wilson, the daughter of a Presbyterian minister. Wilson was proud of his Scotch Presbyterian forebears, and his pride in them doubtless influenced his own career and perhaps the course of history. Wilson graduated from Princeton in 1879, and was admitted to the bar in 1882, after graduating in law from the University of Virginia. He practiced law only briefly before undertaking graduate studies in political science at the Johns Hopkins University, where he received the Ph.D. in 1886. He then entered on an academic career at Bryn Mawr, Wesleyan, and Princeton, where he was elected President in 1902. In the so-called "Battle of Princeton," a bitter struggle concerning academic policies, Wilson lost to Dean Andrew F.

West. Soon thereafter, however, he was elected (1910) Governor of New Jersey; and in 1912 he was elected President of the United States. He was re-elected in 1916. Wilson's domestic policies, notable in themselves, were overshadowed by the commitment to World War I and to his efforts, following the victory, to establish the League of Nations. On September 26, 1919, while on a speaking tour in behalf of the League of Nations, he suffered a breakdown from which he never entirely recovered, and spent the rest of his term in partial isolation. At the end of his second term as President he retired to his home on S Street, in Washington, where he lived in retirement until his death on February 3, 1924.

The text of Woodrow Wilson's "Responding to the New Call of Duty," is taken from *Responding to the New Call of Duty: Addresses of the President, The Secretary of the Navy, and Capt. E. W. Eberle, Superintendent of the Naval Academy, Delivered Before the Graduating Class of the United States Naval Academy at Annapolis, M.D. [sic] on June 2, 1916. Senate Documents, Vol. 43, 64th Congress, 1st Session, December 6, 1915–September 8, 1916* (Washington: Government Printing Office, 1916), pp. 3–4.

The Occasion

If Woodrow Wilson was not the best educated President the United States ever had, he was certainly the most thoroughly schooled. Moreover, unless one counts such tentative adventures in academic life as John Quincy Adams' lectures at Harvard, Wilson was the only professor-president. In a sense Wilson lived in ivory towers at Princeton, at Virginia, at the Hopkins, at Bryn Mawr, at Wesleyan, and again at Princeton until he became Governor of New Jersey in 1910. Wilson was also a Presbyterian—a serious Presbyterian of the covenanting sort—from a long line of Scotch Presbyterians. The influence of the manse as well as of the ivory tower can be observed in Wilson's policies and speeches, including his admonition to the graduates of the U.S. Naval Academy. In his speeches and in his career one may discover both the preacher of the gospel of clean politics and world peace and the professor confident of his truth and impelled to teach it to others.

Perhaps Wilson's indebtedness to the classroom and the pastor's study explains why he was ardently loved and hated, for those who loved him loved him dearly, and those who disliked him did not like him at all. The legend that the senior Senator from Missouri wept in the Senate cloakroom as the Senate voted the declaration of war against Germany in 1917 is not likely to be documented, nor is the language he is said to have used in describing Woodrow Wilson likely to be published. But the legend is true to the fact that Wilson had a great capacity for arousing hatred in those who thought him supercilious, condescending, or insincere. Even William Allen White, who supported all of Wilson's major policies and came eventually to an unshaken belief in his sincerity, once held an unfortunate and unforgettable opinion of him:

He seemed to me hard and repellent. I first met him at Madison, Wisconsin, when he was Governor of New Jersey. I was a fervent believer in his policies, and I came into his presence a hero-worshiper. I had written several editorials supporting his cause which he had seen; which at least he acknowledged. When I met him, he gave me a hand that felt very much like a five-cent mackerel; cold, stiff, moist, unresponsive, extended something as though a clerk desiring a larger sale would casually poke the fish across a counter. He smiled, but I got the wrong side of his face, a side which gave me a certain impression of a reptilian personality—a strong sense of some essential treachery in the man! [1]

Yet Josephus Daniels, who served as Secretary of the Navy throughout both of Wilson's terms in the White House, found no fault in him and quoted with approval Admiral Grayson's estimate of him:

It was my privilege to be Woodrow Wilson's friend as well as his physician, and it would be difficult for me to put in words the affection for him which grew during nearly twelve years of close personal association and confidence.

It will not be for me to express my estimate of his ideals and his character and leadership, nor for me to write his epitaph. Time alone will do that. But in sick days and well, I have never known such single-minded devotion to duty as he saw it against all odds, such

[1] William Allen White, *Woodrow Wilson: The Man, His Times and His Task*, p. xiii.

patience and forbearance with adversity, and finally such resignation to the inevitable. I once read an inscription in a southern country church yard. It said: "He was unseduced by flattery, unawed by opinion, undismayed by disaster. He faced life with antique courage, and death with Christian hope."

Those words, better than any words of mine, describe Woodrow Wilson.[2]

Moreover, one should not lightly dismiss the judgment of Jan Christian Smuts, Prime Minister of South Africa, who was one of the architects of the League of Nations and of the United Nations. Smuts declared: "Hundreds of years hence Wilson's name will be one of the greatest in history."[3]

On June 2, 1916, Woodrow Wilson gave impromptu to the graduating class at the U.S. Naval Academy at Annapolis the address "Responding to the New Call of Duty." In this speech can be observed the covenanter's sense of duty, of respect for obligation. It reveals also the teacher inculcating the thought that boys must be not boys but men. The short speech at Annapolis thus demonstrates as well as any of his longer speeches Wilson's primary gift as rhetorician and orator: the ability so to employ suasive language as to give effect to cherished ideals. The power of his persuasion lay in the clarity of his conceptions and the intensity of his purpose to communicate those conceptions to his hearers.

The Speech

RESPONDING TO THE NEW CALL OF DUTY

MR. SUPERINTENDENT, YOUNG GENTLEMEN, LADIES AND GENTLE-MEN: *It had not been my purpose when I came here to say anything today, but as I sit here and look at you youngsters, I find that my feeling is a very personal feeling indeed. I know some of the things that you have been through and I admire the way in which you have responded to the new call of duty. I*

[2] Josephus Daniels, *The Life of Woodrow Wilson: 1856–1924* (Chicago: The John C. Winston Co., 1924), pp. 342–43.

[3] As cited in Daniels, *op. cit.*, p. 19.

would feel that I had not done either you or myself justice if I did not tell you so.

I have thought that there was one interesting bond that united us. You were at Washington three years ago and saw me get into trouble, and now I am here to see the beginning of your trouble. Your trouble will last longer than mine, but I doubt if it will be any more interesting. I have had a liberal education in the last three years, with which nothing that I underwent before bears the slightest comparison. But what I want to say to you young gentlemen is this: I can illustrate it in this way. Once and again when youngsters here or at West Point have forgotten themselves and done something that they ought not to do and were about to be disciplined, perhaps severely, for it, I have been appealed to by their friends to excuse them from the penalty. Knowing that I have spent most of my life at a college they commonly say to me, "You know college boys. You know what they are. They are heedless youngsters very often, and they ought not to be held up to the same standards of responsibility that older men must submit to." And I have always replied: "Yes; I know college boys. But while these youngsters are college boys, they are something more. They are officers of the United States. They are not merely college boys. If they were, I would look at derelictions of duty on their part in another spirit; but any dereliction of duty on the party of a naval officer of the United States may involve the fortunes of a nation and can not be overlooked." Do you not see the difference? You can not indulge yourselves in weaknesses, gentlemen. You can not forget your duty for a moment, because there might come a time when that weak spot in you should affect you in the midst of a great engagement, and then the whole history of the world might be changed by what you did not do or did wrong.

So that the personal feeling I have for you is this: We are all bound together, I for the time being and you permanently, under a special obligation, the most solemn that the mind can conceive. The fortunes of a nation are confided to us. Now, that ought not to depress a man. Sometimes I think that nothing is worth while that is not hard. You do not improve your muscle by doing the easy thing; you improve it by doing the hard thing, and you get your zest by doing a thing that is difficult, not a thing that is easy. I would a great deal rather, so far as my sense of enjoyment is

CHAPTER 12

I Am Never Guilty

NICOLA SACCO

*I am never guilty, never—not yesterday, nor to-
day nor for ever.*

—NICOLA SACCO

The Speaker

NICOLA SACCO was born in the village of Torremaggiore in
southern Italy on April 22, 1891. With his brother, Sabino Sacco,
he came to the United States and landed in Boston in April,
1908. After working at various jobs of hard labor, Sacco became
a shoe worker. Increasingly conscious of the struggles of laboring
men, he helped to conduct strikes and to share in the responsibilities involved. A philosophical anarchist, Sacco went to Mexico
during World War I to avoid military service.

Sacco was devoted to his wife, Rosina, and to their two children. He had many friends who knew him as a workman, a
family man, and a supporter of labor unions. With one friend in
particular—Bartolomeo Vanzetti—his name has been inextricably
linked by an event that took place in South Braintree, Massachusetts, at about 3:00 P.M., on April 15, 1920. Two men—Parmenter,
a paymaster, and Berardelli, his guard, were shot and killed by
men who seized the payroll of the Slater and Morrill shoe factory
and escaped in an automobile that left the scene of the crime at
high speed.

On September 14, 1920, Sacco and Vanzetti were indicted for the murder of Parmenter and Berardelli. The indictment, the trial that began on May 31, 1921, the verdict of murder in the first degree (reached on July 14, 1921), and subsequent events have continued to be subjects of controversy. Nicola Sacco and Bartolomeo Vanzetti were electrocuted under sentence of death at the Charlestown, Massachusetts, prison on August 23, 1927.

The text of the speech of Nicola Sacco is taken from *The New York Times,* Section 1 (April 10, 1927), p. 26.

The Occasion

The speech of Nicola Sacco was delivered in the courtroom of Judge Webster Thayer in Dedham, Massachusetts, on April 9, 1927, in accordance with the proprieties, long observed in American jurisprudence, that a man condemned to death may speak in his own behalf.[1] Sacco's speech stands out from many other speeches that have been delivered from the courtroom, the scaffold, and the death chamber because of the intense interest in the Sacco-Vanzetti case throughout the United States and in many other parts of the world, and because of the questions still thought to be unresolved concerning the guilt of the accused.

In the annals of protest only the sentence of Dreyfus has approached the Sacco-Vanzetti case in the breadth and the intensity of concern manifested. Doubtless the protest movement was used by international communism as a vehicle for propaganda presumed to demonstrate that a proletarian is unlikely to receive a fair trial in a capitalist nation, but countless individuals and organizations that could not be charged with sympathy for communism wrote, spoke, or demonstrated against the impending execution of Sacco and Vanzetti. They were impelled to act because of their belief in the integrity, as well as of the innocence, of Sacco and Vanzetti, because of prejudice allegedly shown by the trial judge, and because the confession of Celestine Medeiros, who admitted participating in the murder for which Sacco and

---

[1] This statement concerning the Sacco-Vanzetti case is based on dispatches in newspapers contemporary with the event and chiefly on the works listed in the section on further reading.

Vanzetti were condemned, cast such doubt on their conviction as seemed, at least to laymen, to warrant a new trial. Hence demonstrations, protest meetings, and strikes, were held in many states, including New York, New Jersey, Colorado, Illinois, and Pennsylvania. Thousands of Americans, including some opinion leaders, congregated in Boston to protest the "judicial murder." Delegations protested in Bucharest, Berlin, Stockholm, Tokyo, Paris, and Madrid, and throughout the Soviet Union. George Bernard Shaw, H. G. Wells, and Albert Einstein in Europe joined the voices of protest spoken in America by Edna St. Vincent Millay, Sinclair Lewis, Heywood Broun, and many others. The American Civil Liberties Union and the American Federation of Labor interceded in behalf of the condemned men. The protests did not affect the actions of the court, unless perhaps to confirm a judgment already made, for in the climate of feeling existing in the United States in 1927, the support of international communism may have given Sacco and Vanzetti an added burden of proof. Some sections of public opinion were outspoken in declaring their support of the condemnation.

The question of guilt or innocence is unlikely ever to be settled beyond doubt. Three undisputed facts lend support to the argument that the men were guilty as charged:

1. Both men were armed when they were arrested.

2. Their defense was heard by twelve men chosen under procedures normal in American courts of justice. The jury heard the evidence and pronounced them guilty.

3. The case was reviewed by an advisory committee appointed for his guidance by Governor Fuller. The appointment and service of the committee may reasonably be construed as done in good faith and beyond the requirements of statute. Whatever the human limitations of the members of the Committee, and the difficulties imposed on them, they were free agents and presumably, like the jury, they could have brought in a recommendation for commutation of sentence. They did not do so.

On the other hand, there are at least three reasons for believing that Sacco and Vanzetti were not guilty of the crime with which they were charged:

1. The prejudice of Judge Thayer against the accused and their counsel seems established beyond a reasonable doubt. Although it be admitted that the prejudice of the judge does not establish

the innocence of the accused, the prejudice does suggest a conviction without the full benefit of a fair trial.

2. Sacco and Vanzetti were indicted and tried at a time when
public opinion in the United States was aroused against "reds,"
"anarchists," "communists," and "aliens." It was a time of 100
percent, or even 200 percent, Americanism. It is reasonable to
suppose that the prejudices against the "un-American" opinions
of Sacco and Vanzetti admitted by the judge were held in some
degree by members of the jury as well, and that these prejudices
infected the verdict.

3. On the record, as shown in their writings and speeches,
Sacco and Vanzetti do not have the character of murderers. Each
man, in his own way, conveys to a layman the impression that
he is not the kind of person to kill a fellow-creature for money.
If it be objected that laymen are not the proper judges in such
matters, one need only recall that the statutes require laymen to
serve as jurors.

Thoughtful citizens not versed in the law but troubled about
the law's perplexities may come, without deciding the prime
question of guilt or innocence, to the conclusion the *Boston
Herald* pronounced in an editorial on October 26, 1926:

> In our opinion, Nicola Sacco and Bartolomeo Vanzetti ought not to
> be executed on the warrant of the verdict returned by a jury on July
> 14, 1921. . . . We have read the full decision in which Judge Web-
> ster Thayer, who presided at the original trial, renders his decision
> against the application for a new trial, and submit that it carries the
> tone of the advocate rather than the arbitrator.[2]

Forty years after the event, what is a layman in the law to
conclude concerning the death of Sacco and Vanzetti? Confronted with the opinion of William Howard Taft,[3] who evidently
believed Sacco and Vanzetti guilty, and with the judgment of
Felix Frankfurter,[4] who clearly thought them innocent, the layman is likely to resort to the Scotch verdict, *Not Proven,* and to
reflect on the hazards inherent in any system of jurisprudence.

---

[2] As quoted in Felix Frankfurter, *The Case for Sacco and Vanzetti,* p.
115.

[3] Letter, William Howard Taft to Robert A. Grant, as quoted in Joughin
and Morgan, *The Legacy of Sacco and Vanzetti,* p. 38.

[4] Frankfurter, *The Case for Sacco and Vanzetti, passim.*

Whether innocent or guilty, Bartolomeo Vanzetti spoke eloquently not only in the courtroom of Judge Webster Thayer but to a world-wide audience:

This is what I say: I would not wish to a dog or to a snake, to the most low and misfortune creature of the earth—I would not wish to any of them what I have had to suffer for things that I am not guilty of. I am suffering because I am a radical, and indeed I am a radical; I have suffered because I was an Italian, and indeed I am an Italian; I have suffered more for my family and for my beloved than for myself; but I am so convinced to be right that you could execute me two times, and if I could be reborn two other times I would live again to do what I have done already. I have finished; thank you.[5]

Whether innocent or guilty, Nicola Sacco did not cease to speak on April 9, 1927, but continues to say to thoughtful men the speech he gave on that day.

The Speech

I AM NEVER GUILTY

Yes, sir. I am not an orator. It is not very familiar with me, the English language, and as I know, as my friend has told me, my comrade, Vanzetti will speak more long, so I thought to give him the chance.

I never know, never heard, even read in history anything so cruel as this court. After seven years prosecuting they still consider us guilty. And these gentle people here are arrayed with us in this court today.

I know the sentence will be between two classes, the oppressed class and the rich class, and there will be always collision between one and the other. We fraternize the people with the books, with the literature. You persecute the people, tyrannize over them and kill them. We try the education of people always. You try to put a path between us and some other nationality that hates each other. That is why I am here today on this bench, for having been the oppressed class. Well. You are the oppressor.

You know it, Judge Thayer. You know all my life. You know

[5] Special dispatch to *The New York Times*, April 9, 1927.

why I have been here, and after seven years, we that you have been persecuting, me and my poor wife, and you still today sentence us to death. I would like to tell all my life, but what is the use? You know all about what I say before, and my friend—that is, my comrade—will be talking because he is more familiar with the language, and I will give him a chance.

My comrade, the kind man, the kind man to all the child, you sentence him two times, in the Bridgewater case and the Dedham case, connected with me, and you know he is innocent. You forget all this population that has been with us for seven years, to sympathize and give us all their energy and all their kindness. You do not care for them.

Among that peoples and the comrades and the working class there is a big legion of intellectual people which have been with us for seven years, not to commit the iniquitous sentence, but still the Court goes ahead. And I think I thank you all, you peoples, my comrades who have been with me for seven years, with the Sacco-Vanzetti case, and I will give my friend a chance.

I forgot one thing which my comrade remember me. As I said before, Judge Thayer know all my life, and he know that I am never guilty, never—not yesterday, nor today nor for ever.

Further Reading

Inasmuch as the Sacco-Vanzetti case was a celebrated one that aroused passions in the United States and around the world, it developed a great body of polemics as well as some dispassionate inquiry and report. Of the materials readily available concerning the case, the following may be recommended: Michael A. Musmanno, *After Twelve Years* (New York: Alfred A. Knopf, 1939); David Felix, *Sacco-Vanzetti and the Intellectuals* (Bloomington: Indiana University Press, 1965); Eugene Lyons, *The Life and Death of Sacco and Vanzetti* (New York: International Publishers, 1927); Felix Frankfurter, *The Case of Sacco and Vanzetti: A Critical Analysis for Lawyers and Laymen* (Boston: Little, Brown and Co., 1927); and G. Louis Joughin and Edmund M. Morgan, *The Legacy of Sacco and Vanzetti* (New York: Harcourt, Brace and Company, 1948).

A transcript of the record is available in five volumes to a total of 5621 pages, plus an ancillary volume, in *The Sacco-Vanzetti Case: Transcript of the Record of the Trial of Nicola Sacco and Bartolomeo Vanzetti in the Courts of Massachusetts and Subsequent Proceedings* (New York: Harcourt, Brace & Company, 1927–1929), 6 vols. Also available is the record of public hearings on a resolution for posthumous pardon: *Record of Public Hearing Before Joint Committee of the Massachusetts Legislature on the Resolution of Representative Alexander J. Cella Recommending a Posthumous Pardon for Nicola Sacco and Bartolomeo Vanzetti* (Boston: Committee for the Vindication of Sacco and Vanzetti, 1959).

CHAPTER 13

Immigrants and Revolutionists

FRANKLIN D. ROOSEVELT

Remember, remember always that all of us, and you and I especially, are descended from immigrants and revolutionists.

—FRANKLIN D. ROOSEVELT

The Speaker

FRANKLIN DELANO ROOSEVELT, thirty-first President of the United States, was born at Hyde Park, New York, on January 30, 1882. As he indicates in his speech to the Daughters of the American Revolution, his ancestors were among the early European arrivals in America. He attended Groton, Harvard (B.A., 1904), and Columbia. He entered politics, after a brief experience in the practice of law, in 1910 when, after a vigorous campaign, he was elected to the Senate of the state of New York. An early supporter of Woodrow Wilson in 1912, he was chosen as Assistant Secretary of the Navy under the Secretary, Josephus Daniels. In 1920 he was nominated by the Democratic Party for the vice-presidency, as running mate with James M. Cox, in an election won by Harding and Coolidge. The following year Roosevelt was stricken with poliomyelitis. Although he was paralyzed from the waist down, he eventually recovered partial use of his legs and a mastery of the handicap that enabled him to

93

conduct a vigorous campaign for nomination and election to the Governorship of the state of New York (1928) and to the Presidency of the United States for an unprecedented four terms. The depression that had begun during the administration of Herbert Hoover was in full force when Roosevelt first took office in 1932. In an effort to improve the lot of farmers, small business men, and the underprivileged generally, he immediately projected measures that came to be known collectively as the New Deal. He was reelected in 1936 by an overwhelming majority and, with the war in Europe under way, he ran again in 1940 and was reelected. Again in 1944, with the war in progress against Germany and Japan, he was reelected and served until his death on April 12, 1945. Roosevelt's policies, as well as his personality, have been and are the subject of intense and sometimes bitter debate by partisans. However, no one denies him consummate ability as a political leader and as an effective spokesman for the causes he espoused.

The text of Franklin D. Roosevelt's speech to the Daughters of the American Revolution is taken from Item 53 of *The Public Papers and Addresses of Franklin D. Roosevelt with a Special Introduction and Explanatory Notes by President Roosevelt* (New York: The Macmillan Co., 1941), 1938 Volume, pp. 258–60.

The Occasion

When Franklin D. Roosevelt appeared before the Continental Congress of the Daughters of the American Revolution in Washington, D. C. on April 21, 1938, every member, delegate, and guest entitled to a ticket is said to have been on hand.[1] Some 4,000 persons heard him explain why he had not spoken at some earlier Congress. "It isn't the time it takes to come before you and speak for half an hour," he said, "it is the preparation for that half-hour." [2] President Roosevelt then proceeded to speak,

[1] The statement concerning President Franklin D. Roosevelt's speech before the Daughters of the American Revolution is based on the works listed in the section on further reading and on newspaper accounts contemporary with the speech, especially the dispatches to *The New York Times* of April 22, 1938, pp. 1, 9.

[2] *The New York Times,* April 22, 1938, p. 2.

as he said, "without preparation." Yet, even though he had not spent the ten hours of formal preparation that he normally required of himself for a half-hour speech, he was not without the kind of preparation that comes from education and experience. In his boyhood at Groton School he had been active in debating, a learning experience that he always prized. In his undergraduate days at Harvard University he had spent a full academic year in the study of public speaking under the tutelage of Professor George Pierce Baker, one of the foremost teachers of public speaking of his day. After graduating from Harvard, Roosevelt had spent three years in the study of law at Columbia University and three years thereafter in a rather casual practice of law before entering into politics. In 1938 he had spent some 28 years —save for the years of his illness—in the experience of government service and practical politics that required speechmaking. As State Senator, Assistant Secretary of the Navy, Candidate for the Vice-Presidency, Governor of New York, and President of the United States he had many opportunities to practice the art he had studied at Groton and Harvard. He was thus prepared to address any audience without arrogance or fear but with the insight and good humor that come from self-confidence.

Nevertheless, President Roosevelt was not deprecating the need for specific preparation nor misleading his hearers concerning the time he normally required for a serious speech. He knew that, as his successor in the presidency observed, to make a speech is to make policy; and his "Speech Materials" files support the testimony of his secretaries and speech counselors that he took speech preparation very seriously indeed.

When President Roosevelt spoke of his difficulty in finding time to make formal preparation for a speech, he spoke the truth. On the same day that he spoke to the Daughters of the American Revolution in the afternoon, he talked off the record to the American Society of Newspaper Editors in the evening. During the day he conferred with Senator William E. Borah on problems of monopoly and neutrality; and he discussed with Francis E. Townsend—in a conference that was scheduled for five minutes and lasted for thirty—the Townsend Plan for Old Age Revolving Pensions, as well as Townsend's proposal for a coalition government. He received Townsend's thanks for a presidential pardon that had kept Townsend out of jail under a citation for contempt of Congress, and an invitation—with a plaque—from the Thousand Islands Bridge Authority to attend the opening ceremonies for a new bridge.

Not immediate, perhaps, but still pressing for his attention was the business of the Congress. The Senate was debating a bill for expanding the Navy, a measure under attack by Senator Vandenberg; and certain Senators were criticizing the appointments to the TVA Investigating Committee, a matter in which the Executive Branch of the Government had more than a passing interest. The House of Representatives had just passed a nonmilitary supply bill for $220,634,725.00, had received a minority committee report on the Copeland-Lea Pure Food Bill, had heard Representative Taber criticize President Roosevelt's Recovery Plan, and had received Representative Maverick's bill for a national aeronautics academy.[3]

Perhaps apparently a bit less urgent than the business of the Congress, in which the President perforce maintained an interest, were the actions of Hitler in Germany and Mussolini in Italy—while England slept hardly hearing the alarms sounded by Winston Churchill.

April 21, 1938, was thus a busy day during which Franklin Roosevelt took time out to appear before a group that had, less than twenty-four hours earlier, adopted resolutions inferentially condemning all of his policies—except the recommendation for a great expansion in the navy.[4] He gained from the group both laughter and applause.

The Speech

IMMIGRANTS AND REVOLUTIONISTS

I couldn't let a fifth year go by without coming to see you. I must ask you to take me just as I am, in a business suit [exploding flashlight bulb]—and I see you are still in favor of national defense—take me as I am, with no prepared remarks. You know, as a matter of fact, I would have been here to one of your conventions in prior years—one or more—but it is not the time that

[3] *Ibid.*
[4] *Ibid.*, p. 3.

it takes to come before you and speak for half an hour, it is the preparation for that half-hour. And I suppose that for every half-hour speech that I make before a convention or over the radio, I put in ten hours preparing it.

So I have to ask you to bear with me, to let me just come here without preparation to tell you how glad I am to avail myself of this opportunity, to tell you how proud I am, as a Revolutionary descendant, to greet you.

I thought of preaching on a text, but I shall not. I shall only give you the text and I shall not preach on it. I think I can afford to give you the text because it so happens, through no fault of my own, that I am descended from a number of people who came over in the Mayflower. More than that, every one of my ancestors on both sides—and when you go back four generations or five generations it means thirty-two or sixty-four of them —every single one of them, without exception, was in this land in 1776. And there was only one Tory among them.

The text is this: Remember, remember always that all of us, and you and I especially, are descended from immigrants and revolutionists.

I am particularly glad to know that today you are making this fine appeal to the youth of America. To these rising generations, to our sons and grandsons and great-grandsons, we cannot overestimate the importance of what we are doing in this year, in our own generation, to keep alive the spirit of American democracy. The spirit of opportunity is the kind of spirit that has led us as a nation—not as a small group but as a nation—to meet the very great problems of the past.

We look for a younger generation that is going to be more American than we are. We are doing the best that we can and yet we can do better than that, we can do more than that, by inculcating in the boys and girls of this country today some of the underlying fundamentals, the reasons that brought our immigrant ancestors to this country, the reasons that impelled our Revolutionary ancestors to throw off a fascist yoke.

We have a great many things to do. Among other things in this world is the need of being very, very certain, no matter what happens, that the sovereignty of the United States will never be impaired.

There have been former occasions, conventions of the Daugh-

*ters of the American Revolution, when voices were raised, needed
to be raised, for better national defense. This year, you are raising
those same voices and I am glad of it. But I am glad also that the
Government of the United States can assure you today that it is
taking definite, practical steps for the defense of the Nation.*

Further Reading

The texts of Franklin Roosevelt's speeches may be found, for the
most part, in Samuel I. Rosenman, compiler, *The Public Papers
and Addresses of Franklin D. Roosevelt* (New York: Vols. 1–5,
Random House, 1938; Vols. 6–9, The Macmillan Co., 1941; Vols.
10–13, Harper & Brothers Publishers, 1950). The first volume includes a special introduction by Franklin Roosevelt. The three
volumes of biography by Frank Freidel are the obvious source for
a consecutive account of Roosevelt's life. See especially *Franklin
D. Roosevelt: The Apprenticeship* (Boston: Little, Brown and
Co., 1952). For a critical study of Roosevelt as a speechmaker,
one may consult Earnest Brandenburg and Waldo W. Braden,
"Franklin Delano Roosevelt," in Marie K. Hochmuth (ed.), *A
History and Criticism of American Public Address,* Vol. III, pp.
458–530. This study includes (pp. 528–30) a serviceable selected
bibliography.

CHAPTER 14

Blood, Toil, Tears, and Sweat

WINSTON CHURCHILL

> *I would say to the House, as I said to those who*
> *have joined this Government: "I have nothing to*
> *offer but blood, toil, tears, and sweat."*
>
> —WINSTON CHURCHILL

The Speaker

SIR WINSTON CHURCHILL, British orator and statesman, was born at Blenheim Palace on November 30, 1874, and died in London on January 24, 1965. He was the son of Lord Randolph Churchill and of the former Miss Jennie Jerome, of New York City. His mother numbered among her forebears an Iroquois Indian, from whom, as well as from his Anglo-Saxon ancestors, it has sometimes been surmised that Churchill inherited some of his sterner qualities. After a somewhat difficult experience in schools, Churchill entered Sandhurst, the Royal Military College, and then (in 1895) became a subaltern in the British army. On leave from the army, he went to Cuba as a war correspondent and thus began a vocation as newspaperman, journalist, and author that sustained him during the rest of his life and took him to India, to Egypt, and to South Africa in ventures sometimes combining journalism with soldiering.

In 1900 Churchill was elected to Parliament from Oldham, thus beginning his life-long career in politics that led him successively to be Under-Secretary for the Colonies, President of the Board of Trade, Home Secretary, First Lord of the Admiralty, Minister of Munitions, Secretary for War and Air Minister, Chancellor of the Exchequer, and eventually, in 1940, Prime Minister of Great Britain. In the estimation of many persons, British and American, Churchill ranks with Chatham as one of the foremost orator-statesmen produced by the English people.

The text of Churchill's famous speech on taking office as Prime Minister will be found in "His Majesty's Government," *Parliamentary Debates: Fifth Series, House of Commons: Fifth Session of the Thirty-Seventh Parliament of the United Kingdom of Great Britain and Northern Ireland: 4 George VI: Sixth Volume of Session, 1939–40 (This volume may be cited as 360 H.C. Deb. 5 s.), Comprising Period from Tuesday, 23 April to Monday, 13 May, 1940* (London: H. M. Stationery Office, 1940), 1501.

The Occasion

Winston Churchill's speech here reported occurred in regular order of business, under the normal parliamentary procedures of the House of Commons, when on May 13, 1940, Mr. Churchill, as the new Prime Minister, moved the adoption of the following motion:

> That this House welcomes the formation of a Government representing the united and inflexible resolve of this nation to prosecute the war with Germany to a victorious conclusion.[1]

The Prime Minister spoke in behalf of his own motion and was followed immediately by Mr. Lees-Smith of Keighley, who had been asked by his colleagues "on this occasion to follow the Prime Minister because it is fitting that there should be a response to the striking, stirring and noble words which he addressed to the nation." [2] Mr. Lees-Smith assured the House that he and his colleagues supported the Motion, which everyone understood to be the warrant for a coalition government of all

[1] *Parliamentary Debates, op. cit.,* 1501.
[2] *Ibid.*

parties. But not all the speakers who followed Mr. Lees-Smith were quite felicitous in approval of the Motion. Of the twenty-one other members who spoke in debate, either in short comment or at some length, some obviously were sympathetic to the embarrassment of the former Prime Minister, Mr. Chamberlain, who had been required to give up his post of leadership; others (Stafford Cripps, for example) were not satisfied that all issues could be deliberated without adequate provision for His Majesty's Opposition; and Mr. Maxton, the member for Glasgow, Bridgeton, was highly critical of the policies of the Conservative Party, of which Mr. Churchill was an acknowledged if somewhat unruly member. Mr. Maxton doubted the wisdom of leaving the fate of the nation largely in the hands of the party that had presided over the disastrous policies of the past. But the discontents expressed found no single effective voice. Doubtless no action could have satisfied fully every member of the House— Liberal, Labor, Conservative, and Independent—and doubtless the Member for Caernarvon Boroughs, Mr. David Lloyd George, the former Prime Minister and the Senior Member of the House, came as near as anyone could to expressing the preponderant sentiment. In a short speech supporting the motion, he said:

We know the right hon. Gentleman's glittering intellectual gifts, his dauntless courage, his profound study of war, and his experience in its operation and direction. They will all be needed now. I think it is fortunate that he should have been put in a position of supreme authority.

He is exercising his supreme responsibility at a graver moment and in times of greater jeopardy than have ever confronted a British Minister for all time. We all, from the bottom of our hearts, wish him well. The friends of freedom and of human right throughout the world will wish him Godspeed; their hopes are centred in him now because it will depend on him more than on any of his associates. I am not criticizing now, because the man who has got the supreme direction is the man upon whom most of the responsibility depends. May I say that their prayers will be for him and that, in my judgment, the sacrifices of Britain and her Empire will be at his disposal.[3]

At the conclusion of the debate, the House divided with 381 members supporting the Prime Minister's motion and none op-

[3] *Ibid.*, 1510–11.

posed. The House adjourned at 4:36 P.M., having been in session
less than two hours, and Winston Churchill proceeded to complete the formation of a coalition dedicated to his announced
policy "to wage war, by sea, land and air, with all our might
and with all the strength that God can give us. . . ." [4]

The Speech

BLOOD, TOIL, TEARS AND SWEAT

*On Friday evening last I received His Majesty's Commission
to form a new Administration. It was the evident wish and will
of Parliament and the nation that this should be conceived on
the broadest possible basis and that it should include all parties,
both those who supported the late Government and also the parties of the Opposition. I have completed the most important part
of this task. A War Cabinet has been formed of five Members,
representing, with the Opposition Liberals, the unity of the
nation. The three party Leaders have agreed to serve, either
in the War Cabinet or in high executive office. The three Fighting Services have been filled. It was necessary that this should
be done in one single day, on account of the extreme urgency
and rigour of events. A number of other positions, key positions,
were filled yesterday, and I am submitting a further list to His
Majesty to-night. I hope to complete the appointment of the
principal Ministers during to-morrow. The appointment of the
other Ministers usually takes a little longer, but I trust that, when
Parliament meets again, this part of my task will be completed,
and that the administration will be complete in all respects.*

*I considered it in the public interest to suggest that the House
should be summoned to meet to-day. Mr. Speaker agreed, and
took the necessary steps, in accordance with the powers conferred upon him by the Resolution of the House. At the end of
the proceedings to-day the Adjournment of the House will be
proposed until Tuesday, 21st May, with, of course, provision for
earlier meeting, if need be. The business to be considered during
that week will be notified to Members at the earliest opportunity.
I now invite the House, by the Motion which stands in my name,*

[4] *Ibid.,* 1501.

to record its approval of the steps taken and to declare its confidence in the new Government.

To form an Administration of this scale and complexity is a serious undertaking in itself, but it must be remembered that we are in the preliminary stage of one of the greatest battles in history, that we are in action at many other points in Norway and in Holland, that we have to be prepared in the Mediterranean, that the air battle is continuous and that many preparations, such as have been indicated by my hon. Friend below the Gangway, have to be made here at home. In this crisis I hope I may be pardoned if I do not address the House at any length to-day. I hope that any of my friends and colleagues, or former colleagues, who are affected by the political reconstruction, will make allowance, all allowance, for any lack of ceremony with which it has been necessary to act. I would say to the House, as I said to those who have joined this Government: "I have nothing to offer but blood, toil, tears and sweat."

We have before us an ordeal of the most grievous kind. We have before us many, many long months of struggle and of suffering. You ask, what is our policy? I will say: It is to wage war, by sea, land and air, with all our might and with all the strength that God can give us; to wage war against a monstrous tyranny, never surpassed in the dark, lamentable catalogue of human crime. That is our policy. You ask, what is our aim? I can answer in one word: It is victory, victory at all costs, victory in spite of all terror, victory, however long and hard the road may be; for without victory, there is no survival. Let that be realised; no survival for the British Empire, no survival for all that the British Empire has stood for, no survival for the urge and impulse of the ages, that mankind will move forward towards its goal. But I take up my task with buoyancy and hope. I feel sure that our cause will not be suffered to fail among men. At this time I feel entitled to claim the aid of all, and I say, "Come then, let us go forward together with our united strength."

Further Reading

In a life that was long and, as he said "not entirely uneventful," Sir Winston Churchill wrote much and was much written about. Of his own published works, *Their Finest Hour*, the second volume of his six-volume series entitled *The Second World War* (Boston: Houghton Mifflin Co., 1949) is most relevant to his speech of May 13, 1940. In the first chapter of *Their Finest Hour* he tells of forming the National Coalition Government and of the reception accorded the announcement of his policy of blood, toil, tears, and sweat. In *A History of the English-Speaking Peoples* (London: Cassell and Co. Ltd., 1956–1958), 4 vols., Churchill "does not seek to rival the works of professional historians." He aims rather "to present a personal view on the processes whereby English-speaking peoples have achieved their distinctive position and character." Other notable works by Churchill include his biography of his father, *Lord Randolph Churchill* (London: Macmillan and Co., Ltd., 1907) and of his ancestor, *Marlborough: His Life and Times* . . . (New York: Charles Scribner's Sons, 1933–1938), 6 vols.

In *While England Slept: A Survey of World Affairs: 1932–1938* (New York: G. P. Putnam's Sons, 1938) Churchill inveighed against the policies that led Britain to the disasters of 1939–40.

The texts of Churchill's speeches are of course available in documents and in contemporary newspapers. More conveniently some of them can be found in the volumes edited by his son, Randolph Churchill: *Europe Unite: Speeches 1947 and 1948* (Boston: Houghton Mifflin Co., 1950), and *In the Balance* (Boston: Houghton Mifflin Co., 1952).

Of the many books offering accounts of Churchill from varying points of view, the most promising is Randolph Churchill's *Winston S. Churchill* (Boston: Houghton Mifflin Co., 1966), of which the first two volumes have appeared.

Of the books about Churchill, two are primarily concerned with his use of language: Herbert Leslie Stewart, *Sir Winston Churchill as Writer and Speaker* (London: Sidgwick and Jackson, 1954); and Stephen R. Graubard, *Burke, Disraeli and Churchill* (Cambridge: Harvard University Press, 1961).

Those wishing seriously to pursue the life and works of Winston Churchill would do well to consult Frederick Woods, *A Bibliography of the Works of Sir Winston Churchill, KG, OM, CH, MP* (Toronto: University of Toronto Press, 1960).

CHAPTER 15

The Hope of All Mankind
GENERAL DOUGLAS MacARTHUR

It is my earnest hope and indeed the hope of all mankind that from this solemn occasion a better world shall emerge out of the blood and carnage of the past.

GENERAL DOUGLAS MACARTHUR

The Speaker

DOUGLAS MACARTHUR was the son of General Arthur Mac-Arthur, who served with distinction on the side of the North during the Civil War, and of Mary Pinkney Hardy of Virginia, whose brothers fought for the South. He was born in Little Rock, Arkansas, on January 20, 1880. He entered the United States Military Academy at West Point on a Congressional appointment and graduated first in his class in 1903. Commissioned as Second Lieutenant, he was assigned to the Philippines. Later he served in San Francisco and, during the Russo-Japanese War, as aide to his father, who was a military observer. In 1906, Douglas Mac-Arthur served as aide to President Theodore Roosevelt.

MacArthur rose in rank rapidly during World War I, and in June, 1918, was made Brigadier-General. In June, 1919, he was appointed Superintendent of the Military Academy at West Point, where he instituted major changes in the curriculum. Following his tour of duty at West Point, he was assigned to the Philippines, then to be Commander of the Third Corps Area (Baltimore), and then to the Philippines as Commanding General. Thereafter (1930) he was named by President Herbert Hoover as Chief of Staff of the Army, with the rank of General. After five years as Chief of Staff, MacArthur accepted an appointment by President Manuel Quezon as military adviser to the government of the Philippines.

In 1937 General MacArthur married Miss Jean Faircloth. One son was born to them. On his retirement from the United States Army, MacArthur remained in the Philippines; and in July, 1941, as war appeared to be imminent, he was recalled to active duty and appointed to head the forces of the United States in the Far East. On the Japanese invasion of the Philippines, MacArthur was ordered to Australia, where (1942) he was named Supreme Commander in the Southwest Pacific.

Following the expulsion of the Japanese forces from Manila, MacArthur returned to the Philippines and was made General of the Army. When the Japanese surrendered, MacArthur was named Supreme Commander for the Allied Powers and flew to Tokyo to receive the surrender of the Japanese forces.

MacArthur continued as virtual ruler of Japan until he was recalled by President Truman, whereupon he returned to the United States in great public acclaim. He died in New York City on April 5, 1964.

The text of General MacArthur's speech at the surrender ceremonies in Tokyo Bay is taken from "Let Us Pray That Peace Be Now Restored to the World," in *A Soldier Speaks: Public Papers and Speeches of General of the Army Douglas MacArthur* (New York: Frederick A. Praeger, 1965), as edited by Major Vorin E. Whan, Jr., USA. It appears also in *The New York Times* for September 2, 1945. The description of the surrender ceremony given in this chapter is taken from *The New York Times*, September 2, 1945, p. 1.

The Occasion

From its earliest beginnings the American republic has maintained a tradition of epideictic oratory. The opening of a canal, the laying of a cornerstone, the funeral of a notable citizen have traditionally called for a ceremony, usually with a speech thought to be appropriate. At 9:03 on Sunday morning, September 2, 1945, there occurred an event without precedent, yet one that, in accordance with the custom of the country, seemed to call for a ceremony and a speech. The ceremony was conducted and the speech was delivered by General Douglas MacArthur, General of the Army of the United States and newly appointed Supreme Allied Commander.

On board the battleship Missouri anchored in Tokyo Bay some eighteen miles off shore, representatives of His Imperial Majesty, the Emperor of Japan, together with representatives of the Allied Powers, prepared to sign the document attesting the surrender of all Japanese forces. In the ceremony conducted by General MacArthur, the first to sign was Foreign Minister Mamoru Shigemitsu, who signed for the Japanese government; he was followed immediately by General Yoshijiro Umedzu, who signed for the armed forces of Japan. General MacArthur, who then signed as Supreme Commander of the Allied Powers, was attended by General Jonathan Wainwright of Bataan and Corregidor and by Lt. Gen. Sir Arthur E. Percival of Singapore.

In a starkly simple ceremony that required in all only twenty minutes, the representatives of the allied powers stepped forward to sign the acknowledgment of the articles of surrender. The first to sign was Admiral Chester W. Nimitz for the United States of America. He was followed in rapid order by the representatives of China, the United Kingdom, Soviet Russia, Australia, Canada, France, the Netherlands and New Zealand. More than 100 high-ranking military officers observed the proceedings as the flags of the United States, Great Britain, Soviet Russia, and China flew from the deck of the 45,000 ton superdreadnought, *Missouri*. In words of admonition and assurance to the Japanese, General MacArthur delivered the address that was in part ceremonial and in part persuasive to the quiet acceptance of the conditions of surrender by the leaders and the common folk of Japan.

That the speech, and the policies it declared, were effective has been demonstrated not only by events but by Baron Kantaro Suzuki, who was Prime Minister at the time of Japan's surrender:

The last audience I had [with the Emperor] was in the middle of June 1946, when I resigned from the presidency of the Privy Council.

On that occasion His Majesty said to me that the occupation policy of Supreme Commander MacArthur was fair and just, and things were progressing quite satisfactorily. Now with the full realization that I was right in my conviction about trusting in the enemy commander, I am watching from my country place of retirement the operation of the Allied occupation policy and the progress of the democratization of Japan. I am very happy to know that the course on which I chose to steer the nation to the termination of war has proved by no means a bad thing for Japan.[1]

The Speech

THE HOPE OF ALL MANKIND

We are gathered here, representatives of the major warring powers, to conclude a solemn agreement whereby peace may be restored. The issues, involving divergent ideals and ideologies, have been determined on the battlefields of the world and hence are not for our discussion or debate. Nor is it for us here to meet, representing as we do a majority of the peoples of the earth, in a spirit of distrust, malice, or hatred. But rather it is for us, both victors and vanquished, to rise to that higher dignity which alone befits the sacred purposes we are about to serve, committing all of our peoples unreservedly to faithful compliance with the undertakings they are here formally to assume.

It is my earnest hope and indeed the hope of all mankind that from this solemn occasion a better world shall emerge out of the blood and carnage of the past—a world founded upon faith and understanding—a world dedicated to the dignity of man and the fulfillment of his most cherished wish—for freedom, tolerance, and justice.

The terms and conditions upon which surrender of the Japanese Imperial forces is here to be given and accepted are contained in the instrument of surrender now before you.

As Supreme Commander for the Allied Powers I announce it my firm purpose, in the tradition of the countries I represent, to proceed in the discharge of my responsibilities with justice and tolerance, while taking all necessary dispositions to insure that

---

[1] Douglas MacArthur, *Reminiscences*, p. 279.

the terms of surrender are fully, promptly, and faithfully complied with.

I now invite the representatives of the Emperor of Japan and the Japanese Government, and the Japanese Imperial General Headquarters, to sign the instrument of surrender at the places indicated.

The Supreme Commander for the Allied Powers will now sign on behalf of all the nations at war with Japan.

The representative of the United States of America will now sign.

The representative of the Republic of China will now sign.

The representative of the United Kingdom will now sign.

The representative of the Union of Soviet Socialist Republics will now sign.

The representative of Australia will now sign.

The representative of Canada will now sign.

The representative of France will now sign.

The representative of Netherlands will now sign.

The representative of New Zealand will now sign.

Let us pray that peace be now restored to the world, and that God will preserve it always.

These proceedings are closed.

Further Reading

General Douglas MacArthur is still a controversial person about whom diverse views are held and expressed. Perhaps the best book to read first is MacArthur's own *Reminiscences* (New York: McGraw-Hill Book Co., 1964). A number of MacArthur's public statements will be found in *A Soldier Speaks: Public Papers and Speeches of General Douglas MacArthur. The Quarterly Journal of Speech*, XXXVII (October, 1951), presented varying views of his famous address to the Congress in a symposium edited by Frederick W. Haberman. Other volumes likely to be useful to those interested in the general and the orator are Charles A. Willoughby and John Chamberlain, *MacArthur: 1941–1951* (New York: McGraw-Hill Book Co., 1954); Frazier Hunt, *The Untold Story of Douglas MacArthur* (New York: The

Devin-Adair Co., 1954); Richard H. Rovere and Arthur M. Schlesinger, Jr., *The General and the President and the Future of American Foreign Policy* (New York: Farrar, Straus and Young, 1951); John Gunther, *The Riddle of MacArthur* (New York: Harper & Brothers, 1951); John Hersey, *Men on Bataan* (New York: Alfred A. Knopf, 1942); and William J. Sebald and Russell Brines, *With MacArthur in Japan: A Personal History of the Occupation* (New York: W. W. Norton & Co., Inc., 1965).

References to General MacArthur and his policies will be found in a great many publications, particularly for the decade 1941–1951. Perhaps the most noteworthy references appear in Harry S. Truman's *Memoirs* (Garden City, New York: Doubleday & Co., Inc., 1956).

The papers of General MacArthur are now deposited in the MacArthur Memorial at Norfolk, Virginia, where they will doubtless be available to qualified scholars.

CHAPTER 16

The Democratic Faith

DAVID E. LILIENTHAL

*Traditionally, democracy has been an affirmative
doctrine rather than merely a negative one.*

—DAVID E. LILIENTHAL

The Speaker

DAVID ELI LILIENTHAL was born at Morton, Illinois, on July
8, 1899. He received the A.B. degree at DePauw University in
1920 and the LL.B. at Harvard in 1923. The honorary degree,
LL.D., has been conferred on him by a number of universities.
He was admitted to the bar of Illinois in 1923, and practiced
law in Chicago until 1931, when he became a member of the
Wisconsin Public Service Commission. He served as Chairman
of the Tennessee Valley Authority from 1941 to 1946, and as
Chairman of the United States Atomic Energy Commission from
1946 to 1950.

The text of Mr. Lilienthal's speech is taken *verbatim* from the
*Hearings Before the Senate Section of the Joint Committee on
Atomic Energy, Eightieth Congress, First Session, on Confirmation of the Atomic Energy Commission and the General Man-
ager* (Washington: United States Government Printing Office,
1947), pp. 131–32.

The Occasion

On the morning of January 27, 1947, David E. Lilienthal, who
had been nominated as Chairman of the United States Atomic
Energy Commission, appeared before the Senate Section of the
Joint Committee on Atomic Energy of the Eightieth Congress to
undergo inquiry concerning his fitness to hold the post. Although
Senator Kenneth D. McKellar of Tennessee was not a member of
the Committee, he was accorded the privilege of sitting with the
Committee and of interrogating persons brought before it. During
Mr. Lilienthal's administration of the Tennessee Valley Authority,
he had incurred the ill-will of Senator McKellar. The Senator—
not one to forget an injury or a supposed injury—took a leading
part in an attempt to prevent the confirmation of Mr. Lilienthal.
In the entry in his journal for January 27, 1947, Mr. Lilienthal
describes the hearing:

> I wish I could tell now—while it is fresh in my mind—just how
> one feels when he takes the witness chair, with the room rather tensing
> and sniggering about it; or the feeling one has under the Old Man's [1]
> rather baleful look as he leafs through his papers and begins to ask
> questions, questions that usually are speeches directed to the news-
> papers, and which when I answer make him quite impatient—that
> not being what he wants. This hearing is quite different from the usual
> ones with him, however, in this: that the chairman will protect me if
> the Old Boy won't let me answer—his past habit—so I can take my
> time and divide the questions up—he usually puts two or three ques-
> tions into a single one, and with an assumption or two in every one—
> and answer them or deny the assumptions. The record reads very
> well—a good stenographer—but chiefly it reads well because I have
> this assurance that the chairman will give me a chance to say my say
> without harassment.[2]

In his determination to block the nomination of Mr. Lilienthal,
Senator McKellar finally went too far. On February 4, 1947, as
he persisted in a line of questioning of dubious import, the

---

[1] The terms *old man* and *old boy* in Mr. Lilienthal's narrative obviously
refer to Senator McKellar. The Chairman of the investigating committee was
Senator Bourke B. Hickenlooper.

[2] David E. Lilienthal, *The Journals of David E. Lilienthal: Volume II,
The Atomic Energy Years,* p. 138.

Senator moved Mr. Lilienthal to reply with an impromptu statement as distinguished for its clarity as for its insight into the
meaning of the democratic faith. An effective speech, in an
unusual setting, the statement elicited acclaim from Senators,
both Democratic and Republican, and brought Mr. Lilienthal
widespread sympathy and support. Seldom has an impromptu
speech had such an immediate and assured effect. Moreover, as
an impromptu speech it may possibly be unique in the extent
of the documentation concerning it, especially concerning the
speaker's recorded recollections of his own state of mind preceding and at the moment of delivery. These recollections will reward the attention of anyone holding a serious interest in the
processes of speechmaking:

The morning (Tuesday, February 4) was rough; I felt depressed
and tired; my back had been kicking up badly again, and I lay down
for two five-minute periods to ease it up. I lunched in the rather dismal
Interior Department cafeteria, having to stand holding my filled tray
for ten minutes because there were no tables. At 1:45 we started for
the Hill. I was to go on at 2:00.

I sat back in the audience in the rather small hearing room, the
Finance Committee's regular room. President Conant was called, was
photographed, told the committee about Wilson, made a good impression but not a very strong one, I feared. McKellar furnished a bit of
comedy by asking the distinguished scientist if he had heard of the
bomb before Hiroshima, whether he knew that the Macedonians had
tried "to split the atom." Conant said some fine things about me, about
others of the Commission. He left the witness chair. The chairman
called my name.

I pushed my way through the chairs, almost back to back, of the
press table, moved the swivel chair away and put a straight chair in its
place, put down my manila envelope, nodded to the chairman, and
turned to my left to face Senator McKellar, looking down at me from
the height of the "bench" that curves in a half-ellipse around the "victim."

I recall feeling relaxed, the inner cautions against losing my temper
or composure at anything the Old Man might say apparently function-
ing. I used to have a sense of repugnance and in the earliest days even
of dread of the ordeal; none of this now. I looked the Old Man full in
the face. Not a pretty sight, really, but it somehow made it seem
easier. This was about a quarter to three or so. A question about TVA
ammonium nitrate, how much a ton. I thought I knew the answer, but
I knew there was no reason to "recall" something so specific and then

discuss my recollection—no, I didn't try to remember such things. A question returning to the birthplace of my parents, a question he had put on the Friday before. Over the weekend I had tried to locate the paper on which Dad had put the names of the villages where he and Mother were born; Helen couldn't find it at home, and Miss Reames hadn't had time to locate it in the office files we brought along from Tennessee. But by consulting a map at home last Sunday, Pressburg I knew to be the city near which were these villages so that I had written into the transcript—"the vicinity of Pressburg."

The Old Man pressed me on this. I felt trembly inside, with disgust at the meanness that he wasn't quite able to expose fully—only by this snide pretense of interest in knowing where my parents were born. My reply had feeling in it; I was dangerously near anger. He dropped it, and I relaxed and had myself in hand. But I was now aroused, a kind of smolder, far from anger or temper, but some emotional tempo quite different, but definitely emotional. Then, with a pleased look on his face, glancing out at the audience and half-smiling as he put the question—the cat just before the mouse is cornered—the generous complacent look when the victim is about to be taken in hand: some taunt about being leftist—Communist.

The stenographic transcript shows that I talked for several minutes, that what I said consisted of sentences that had subjects, verbs, predicates, that began in an ordinary, rather formal fashion, and marched on to a conclusion, that there was a pattern of word order and tempo. But I was not conscious of sentences or form or sequence at all. I remember a signal: Don't just deny; affirm. I remember that I didn't look at him, but squared myself away directly to the table before me, that I looked down and what I said seemed to me talking to myself. I wasn't conscious of a committeee, and it was so silent, not a sound except my voice, rather low and without emphasis, going on. It was in me, and I was getting it out. McKellar and the hearing were a long, long way away.

I paused, sat back in the chair, unfolded my hands, said, "This I deeply believe," and sat silent. It was dead quiet, and I now was conscious of the quiet. Then a voice from the bench, before me, on the left of the chairman: Senator McMahon in a solemn voice saying something in praise of what I had said. More silence, and I was becoming self-conscious and fidgety. Then the press table, the audience—I could hear sounds and remembered that they were still there. And then McKellar, looking at his papers, asking a question.[3]

[3] David E. Lilienthal, *op. cit.*, pp. 140–42. Reprinted by permission of Harper & Row, and of Mr. David E. Lilienthal.

The Speech

THE DEMOCRATIC FAITH

My convictions are not so much concerned with what I am against as what I am for—and that excludes a lot of things automatically.

Traditionally, democracy has been an affirmative doctrine rather than merely a negative one.

I believe in—and I conceive the Constitution of the United States to rest, as does religion, upon—the fundamental proposition of the integrity of the individual; and that all Government and all private institutions must be designed to promote and protect and defend the integrity and the dignity of the individual; that that is the essential meaning of the Constitution and the Bill of Rights, as it is essentially the meaning of religion.

Any forms of government, therefore, and any other institutions, which make men means rather than ends in themselves, which exalt the state or any other institutions above the importance of men, which place arbitrary power over men as a fundamental tenet of government, are contrary to this conception; and therefore I am deeply opposed to them.

The communistic philosophy, as well as the communistic form of government, falls within this category, for its fundamental tenet is quite to the contrary. The fundamental tenet of communism is that the state is an end in itself, and that therefore the powers which the state exercises over the individual are without any ethical standards to limit them. That I deeply disbelieve.

It is very easy simply to say one is not a Communist. And, of course, if despite my record it is necessary for me to state this very affirmatively, then this is a great disappointment to me. It is very easy to talk about being against communism. It is equally important to believe those things which provide a satisfactory and effective alternative. Democracy is that satisfying affirmative alternative.

And its hope in the world is that it is an affirmative belief, rather than simply a belief against something else, and nothing more.

One of the tenets of democracy that grow out of this central core of a belief that the individual comes first, that all men are the children of God and their personalities are therefore sacred, is a deep belief in civil liberties and their protection; and a repugnance to anyone who would steal from a human being that which is most precious to him, his good name, by imputing things to him, by inuendo, or by insinuation.

And it is especially an unhappy circumstance that occasionally that is done in the name of democracy.

This I think is something that can tear our country apart and destroy it—if we carry it further.

I deeply believe in the capacity of democracy to surmount any trials that may lie ahead provided only we practice it in our daily lives.

And among the things that we must practice is this: that while we seek fervently to ferret out the subversive and anti-democratic forces in the country, we do not at the same time, by hysteria, by resort to inuendo and sneers and other unfortunate tactics, besmirch the very cause that we believe in, and cause a separation among our people, cause one group and one individual to hate another, based upon mere attacks, mere unsubstantiated attacks upon their loyalty.

I want also to add that part of my conviction is based upon my training as an Anglo-American common lawyer. It is the very basis and the great heritage of the English people to this country, which we have maintained, that the strictest rules of credibility of witnesses and of the avoidance of hearsay and gossip shall be excluded in courts of justice.

And that, too, is an essential of our democracy.

And whether by administrative agencies acting arbitrarily against business organizations, or whether by investigating activities of the legislative branches, whenever those principles fail, those principles of the protection of an individual and his good name against besmirchment by gossip, hearsay, and the statements of witnesses who are not subject to cross-examination: then, too, we have failed in carrying forward our ideals in respect to democracy.

This I deeply believe.

Further Reading

As everyone knows, Mr. Lilienthal survived the Hearings before the Senate Committee, was confirmed by the Senate, and served as Chairman of the Atomic Energy Commission from 1946 until 1950. Those interested in Mr. Lilienthal and in his career, in which speechmaking was a significant influence, should read *The Journals of David E. Lilienthal* (Harper & Row), of which Volume I (*The TVA Years: 1939–1945*) and Volume II (*The Atomic Energy Years: 1945–1950*) were published in 1964 and Volume III (*The Venturesome Years: 1950–1955*) in 1966.

Three other works by Mr. Lilienthal deserve mention: *This I Do Believe* (New York: Harper & Brothers, 1949) explicates the theme of Mr. Lilienthal's famous statement made on February 4, 1947, in response to Senator McKellar's questioning. *Big Business: A New Era* (New York: Harper & Brothers, 1952) reflects Mr. Lilienthal's experience as an executive following his service as an administrator of public enterprises. He expresses the conviction that Big Business "represents a proud and fruitful achievement of the American people as a whole." A more recent publication, *Change, Hope and the Bomb* (Princeton, New Jersey: Princeton University Press, 1963) includes some of Mr. Lilienthal's major addresses.

Mr. Lilienthal has not been the subject of a complete and formal biography. However, the late Bishop G. Bromley Oxnam, in a series of lectures delivered at the Drew Theological Seminary, discussed the views and the accomplishments of Mr. Lilienthal under the title, "The Administrator as Social Reformer." This lecture, with the others of the series, appears in Dr. Oxnam's book *Personalities in Social Reform* (New York: Abingdon-Cokesbury Press, 1950). It includes a text of the speech of February 4, 1947, and excerpts from other speeches by Mr. Lilienthal.

CHAPTER 17

Farewell to a Friend

ADLAI E. STEVENSON

I don't know much about the riches of life, and I suspect few of you have found the last definition. But I do know that friendship is the greatest enrichment that I have found.

—ADLAI E. STEVENSON

The Speaker

ADLAI EWING STEVENSON was born in Los Angeles on February 5, 1900. He was named for his grandfather, also Adlai Ewing Stevenson (1835–1914), who was twice a member of Congress from Illinois, and was Vice-President of the United States during Grover Cleveland's second term (1893–1897). Lewis Green Stevenson, son of the Vice-President and father of the younger Adlai E. Stevenson, served by appointment as Secretary of State for Illinois from 1914 to 1916. The younger Adlai Stevenson thus grew up in an atmosphere of party politics. Following his studies at Princeton University, the conferring of his law degree by Northwestern University, and his admission to the Illinois bar (1926) he naturally devoted himself to politics, to law, and to civic affairs.

Stevenson practiced law in Chicago until 1941, when he became special assistant to Frank Knox, Secretary of the Navy.

As one of his duties he assisted Knox in the preparation of speeches. Subsequently, he was assistant to Edward R. Stettinius and later to James F. Byrnes in the Department of State. He served as Adviser to the United States delegation at the San Francisco Conference (1945), as Senior Adviser to the United States delegation at the first session of the United Nations General Assembly in London (1946), and as Alternate Delegate to the General Assemblies in New York (1946 and 1947). In 1948 Stevenson was elected Governor of Illinois. In 1952 and again in 1956 he was the candidate of the Democratic Party for the Presidency of the United States. On the election of John F. Kennedy to the Presidency in 1960, Stevenson accepted appointment as Ambassador of the United States to the United Nations, a position he held when he died in London on July 14, 1965.

The text of Adlai Stevenson's "Farewell to a Friend" is taken from the printed record of the services conducted for Lloyd Lewis at Libertyville, Illinois, on April 23, 1949. The text was loaned to the editors by Mrs. Lloyd Lewis.

The Occasion

Lloyd Lewis was a native of Indiana, a graduate of Swarthmore College, a reporter, a drama critic, an editor (Chicago *Daily News*), a columnist (Chicago *Sun*), a playwright, and an author whose most notable work, *Captain Sam Grant* (Boston: Little, Brown and Co., 1950) was published posthumously. He was also at Libertyville, Illinois, the neighbor of Adlai E. Stevenson, who was Governor of Illinois at the time of the sudden death of Lloyd Lewis in 1949. Just a few hours before he was stricken, Lloyd Lewis had mailed to Adlai Stevenson a gay letter that reached him in Springfield just as he was given the sad news of the death of his friend.[1]

Because Lloyd Lewis' family had been Quakers for several generations, it was decided that his funeral should have the

---

[1] For the statements concerning the funeral services of Lloyd Lewis, and the speeches at the service, the editors are indebted to Elizabeth Stevenson Ives, to Adlai E. Stevenson III, to Marc Connelly, to Carol Evans, and to Kathryn Lewis (Mrs. Lloyd Lewis), who responded generously to inquiries and supplied the information on which this account is based.

simplicity of the Quaker ritual. Two of his closest friends would speak with short periods for meditation after each address and the service would conclude by having two other friends silently shake hands across the coffin. The services were conducted in the garden of the Lewis residence in Libertyville beside the Des Plaines River.

Marc Connelly and Adlai Stevenson were asked to speak, but Stevenson declined with the explanation that he was emotionally not prepared. However, when Marc Connelly had concluded his talk, Adlai Stevenson felt moved to speak and did speak impromptu the words now called "Farewell to a Friend." [2]

Besides Marc Connelly and Adlai Stevenson, among those present at the services were many other friends of Lloyd Lewis, including Claudia Cassidy, who described the occasion in her column:

SO MANY PEOPLE who could not be there have asked about Lloyd Lewis' funeral that I think it will not be out of place if I tell you it was just what it should have been in just tribute of honor and love. It was simple, quiet, beautiful, rich in comforting things to remember.

We drove out to Libertyville in the cool, sunny morning, and as we drew near the private road we found lines of cars parked and people waiting. The thick woods inside permitted little parking space, so the school bus and a private car or two were available to take you in and out. The police were there, but no one rushed about importantly, giving orders. They were friendly and helpful, you might say neighborly.

Inside, the long, low, brown house clung to the earth as Frank Lloyd Wright meant it to cling, and the little river flowed quietly below. Because there were so many of us, the services, of Quaker simplicity, were held in the garden. Flowers were banked high along the sheltered south wall, and at the bier two men spoke. No one told you the first was Marc Connelly, who wrote "The Green Pastures." No one told

---

[2] The preservation of the impromptu remarks of Governor Stevenson is due to the thoughtfulness of Mrs. Louise Wright, who with her husband Professor Quincy Wright, was among the close friends who attended the services. Mrs. Wright, realizing that Sister Mary St. Gerald (sister of Mrs. Lloyd Lewis and a member of the Sisters of Charity of the Blessed Virgin Mary) would not be able to attend the services, had arranged for a public stenographer to be present and to make a record for Sister Mary St. Gerald. Later Mrs. Wright had the stenographic record printed.

you the second was Adlai Stevenson, the governor of Illinois. They were neighbors, who talked quietly of a friend.

The sun shone and there was no music but the high wind that shook the listeners, yet because of the sheltering wall left the flowers still. And tho you could see the necessary microphone, not even that April wind reminded you of its presence. Mike Todd, who was standing beside us, abruptly said, "Lloyd was about the closest to religion I ever got."

Because it all seemed so right, it had not occurred to me that in a Chicago April few gardens bloom. But this is what had happened. The Lewises had just completed a landing place leading from the house down the little bank to the river. The slope was a havoc of excavation, the garden covered with compost. But when the neighbors heard what had happened, they quietly took over. They smoothed the bank and turfed it, they cleared the garden, and everywhere they planted flowers bravely in bloom.

I thought you might want to know this, because to me it is such a lovely thing to remember.[3]

In these circumstances Adlai Stevenson, a master of the word who in his lifetime gave many speeches throughout the United States and abroad, delivered impromptu what was perhaps his most felicitous address.

The Speech

FAREWELL TO A FRIEND

I have been asked to share in these farewells to a friend.

I think it is a good day for this meeting. It is April now and all life is being renewed on the bank of this river that he loved so well. I think we will all be happy that it happened on this day, here by the river with the spring sky so clear, and the west wind so warm and fresh. I think we will all be the better for this day and this meeting together.

He was my neighbor. He was the neighbor of many of you. He was a very good neighbor; quick in time of misfortune, always present in times of mirth and happiness—and need.

[3] Claudia Cassidy, "On the Aisle," *Chicago Sunday Tribune*, May 1, 1949. Reprinted, courtesy of the *Chicago Tribune*.

I think Mr. Connelly was right when he said he was the most successful man he ever knew. I don't know much about the riches of life, and I suspect few of you have found the last definition. But I do know that friendship is the greatest enrichment that I have found.

Everyone loved this man. He enriched others and was enriched. Everyone was his friend—everyone who knew him or read him. Why was that? Why is he the most successful man that many of us will ever know? Our answers will differ. For me it was his humility, gentleness, wisdom and wit, all in one. And most of all a great compassionate friendliness.

I think it will always be April in our memory of him. It will always be a bright, fresh day, full of the infinite variety and the promise of new life. Perhaps nothing has gone at all—perhaps only the embodiment *of the thing—tender, precious to all of us— a friendship that is immortal and doesn't pass along. It will be renewed for me, much as I know it will for all of you, each spring.*

Further Reading

With Walter Johnson as editor and Carol Evans as assistant editor, the papers of Adlai E. Stevenson are now being edited at the University of Hawaii for publication by the University of Chicago Press. Doubtless a definitive biography of Mr. Stevenson will be forthcoming in due course. Meanwhile, the following titles by Stuart Gerry Brown are recommended: *Conscience in Politics: Adlai E. Stevenson in the 1950's* (Syracuse, New York: Syracuse University Press, 1961), and *Adlai E. Stevenson: A Short Biography: The Conscience of the Country* (Woodbury, New York: Barron's Woodbury Press, 1965). *My Brother Adlai* (New York: William Morrow & Co., 1956), by Elizabeth Stevenson Ives and Hildegarde Dolson, is a lively ancedotal account of Stevenson from childhood to the year of his second campaign for the presidency. Other volumes, more recent, are by Alden Whitman and *The New York Times, Portrait: Adlai E. Stevenson: Politician, Diplomat, Friend* (New York: Harper & Row, 1965); and by Lillian Ross, *Adlai Stevenson* (Philadelphia: J. B. Lippincott Co., 1966).

The texts of Stevenson's speeches, on which he normally

lavished care, are available in a number of volumes, of which the following may be suggested: *Major Campaign Speeches of Adlai E. Stevenson: 1952* (New York: Random House, 1953); *Putting First Things First: A Democratic View* (New York: Random House, 1960); and *Looking Outward* (New York: Harper & Row, 1963). *Call to Greatness* (New York: Harper & Brothers, 1954) provides the text of the Godkin lectures delivered at Harvard in 1954.

CHAPTER **18**

On Accepting the Nobel
Prize for Literature

WILLIAM FAULKNER

*I believe that man will not merely endure: he will
prevail.*

—WILLIAM FAULKNER

The Speaker

WILLIAM FAULKNER was born near Oxford, Mississippi, on
September 25, 1897. His family, once distinguished, fell on evil
days—as did many others in the South—following the Civil War.
Faulkner grew up in the worst kind of poverty—the genteel
sort practiced by those who have known better days. He had
almost no formal education beyond the grammar school. Most
of his early education was obtained from his grandfather's mod-
erate though reasonably diffuse and catholic library. During
World War I he volunteered for service with the Royal Cana-
dian Air Force and served as a pilot. After the war he returned
to Oxford, Mississippi, and to a variety of odd jobs. He left
Mississippi for journeys to New Orleans, to New York, and to
Europe, but returned to undertake the career as novelist and
short story writer that consumed the remainder of his life.
Faulkner died in Oxford, Mississippi, on July 6, 1962.

The text of William Faulkner's speech is taken, by permission
of Random House, Inc., from *The Faulkner Reader: Selections*

from the Works of William Faulkner (New York: Random House, Inc., 1953), pp. 3–4.

The Occasion

William Faulkner was not an orator. Indeed he seems rarely to have appeared in public either as lecturer or speaker. He was rather a poet who wrote novels of a kind new to American fiction, novels resembling those of Dostoevski in their view of the futility, the tragedy, and sometimes the buffoonery of mankind upon a dismal planet. His novels, perhaps more respected abroad than in the United States, have evoked widely differing responses among his fellow-Americans, including his kinsmen in the South inhabited by the families of Sartoris and Snopes. Faulkner has been charged with deliberate and verbose obscurantism, but anyone who has survived the struggle for existence in his mythical Yoknapatawpha County, Mississippi, is unlikely ever to be quite the same again. Upon those who can read him, Faulkner's novels have a profound effect.

Sometimes thought to be a nihilist, a pessimist, a bitter detractor of the human race, Faulkner amazed his countrymen on December 10, 1950, when he delivered his now famous speech accepting the Nobel Prize for Literature. Against the background of Faulkner's novels and short stories in which the central characters were as often as not the deluded, the dispossessed, the neurotic females and the castrated males of a sickly country, Faulkner's strong affirmation of faith in humankind came as a distinct surprise even to some of his admirers who had enjoyed his presumed low opinion of the human race. A close reading of Faulkner, however, discloses in even the most pitiless of his accounts of the human struggle (for instance, in *As I Lay Dying*) the central thesis that man is a courageous, an enduring creature, destined to survive. Hence the Speech of Acceptance need not be read as out of character. If it represents a different Faulkner, it represents one different only in form, in a straightforward discourse of clarity not adopted in his novels. The speech can hardly be misunderstood. Let it speak for itself.

The Speech

ON ACCEPTING THE NOBEL PRIZE FOR LITERATURE

I feel that this award was not made to me as a man, but to my work—a life's work in the agony and sweat of the human spirit, not for glory and least of all for profit, but to create out of the materials of the human spirit something which did not exist before. So this award is only mine in trust. It will not be difficult to find a dedication for the money part of it commensurate with the purpose and significance of its origin. But I would like to do the same with the acclaim too, by using this moment as a pinnacle from which I might be listened to by the young men and women already dedicated to the same anguish and travail, among whom is already that one who will some day stand here where I am standing.

Our tragedy today is a general and universal physical fear so long sustained by now that we can even bear it. There are no longer problems of the spirit. There is only the question: When will I be blown up? Because of this, the young man or woman writing today has forgotten the problems of the human heart in conflict with itself which alone can make good writing because only that is worth writing about, worth the agony and the sweat.

He must learn them again. He must teach himself that the basest of all things is to be afraid; and, teaching himself that, forget it forever, leaving no room in his workshop for anything but the old verities and truths of the heart, the old universal truths lacking which any story is ephemeral and doomed—love and honor and pity and pride and compassion and sacrifice. Until he does so, he labors under a curse. He writes not of love but of lust, of defeats in which nobody loses anything of value, of victories without hope and, worst of all, without pity or compassion. His griefs grieve on no universal bones, leaving no scars. He writes not of the heart but of the glands.

Until he relearns these things, he will write as though he stood among and watched the end of man. I decline to accept the end of man. It is easy enough to say that man is immortal simply because he will endure: that when the last ding-dong of doom has clanged and faded from the last worthless rock hanging tideless in the last red and dying evening, that even then there will still be one more sound: that of his puny inexhaustible voice, still talking. I refuse to accept this. I believe that man will not merely endure: he will prevail. He is immortal, not because he alone among creatures has an inexhaustible voice, but because he has a soul, a spirit capable of compassion and sacrifice and endurance. The poet's, the writer's, duty is to write about these things. It is his privilege to help man endure by lifting his heart, by reminding him of the courage and honor and hope and pride and compassion and pity and sacrifice which have been the glory of his past. The poet's voice need not merely be the record of man, it can be one of the props, the pillars to help him endure and prevail.

Further Reading

Even before, but increasingly since his death, William Faulkner has been the subject of appraisal, of criticism, and of reviews. No satisfying account of his life has yet appeared; doubtless one will be forthcoming in the future. Meanwhile those who are intrigued by his novels, or by his acceptance speech, or by the apparent discrepancy between them, would do well to turn to his fiction and read it in the light of the acceptance speech. Perhaps a good place to begin is with *The Bear,* a novella more conventional in some respects than the longer narratives. *Old Man* is a credible story told authoritatively in Mississippi vernacular. *Sound and Fury* is thought by some Faulknerians to be his best novel. All of these works are to be found in *The Faulkner Reader* (New York: Random House, Inc., 1953), which also includes a foreword by Faulkner, a number of his short stories, and the text of his Nobel Prize address. Further insight into Faulkner's views can be gained from James B. Meriwether (ed.), *Essays, Speeches & Public Letters by William Faulkner* (New York: Random House, Inc., 1965).

CHAPTER 19

Ich bin ein Berliner

JOHN F. KENNEDY

*All free men, wherever they may live, are citizens
of Berlin, and, therefore, as a free man, I take pride
in the words "Ich bin ein Berliner."*

—JOHN F. KENNEDY

The Speaker

JOHN FITZGERALD KENNEDY, the son of Joseph P. Kennedy
and Rose Fitzgerald Kennedy, was born in Boston on May 29,
1917. He attended the public schools in Brookline, as well as
the Canterbury School and the Choate School. He attended the
London School of Economics, Stanford University, and Princeton
University, as well as Harvard University, where he graduated
cum laude in 1940. During World War II he served in the United
States Navy. Injured in the line of duty, he was awarded the
Purple Heart, as well as the Navy and Marine Corps Medal. He
was elected to the United States House of Representatives, and
served in the Eightieth, Eighty-First, and Eighty-Second Con-
gresses prior to his election to the United States Senate from
Massachusetts in 1952. He assumed the Presidency of the United
States on January 20, 1961. On November 22, 1963, President
Kennedy was assassinated. He is buried in the Arlington National
Cemetery.

The text of "Ich bin ein Berliner" is taken from item 269, "Remarks in the Rudolphe Wilde Platz, Berlin, June 26, 1963, in *Public Papers of the Presidents of the United States: John F. Kennedy: Containing the Public Messages, Speeches, and Statements of the President: January 1 to November 22, 1963* (Washington, D. C.: United States Government Printing Office, 1964), pp. 525–52.

The Occasion

One of the gravest disasters ever experienced in the conduct of American foreign policy, and the most obvious error of the Kennedy administration, was the invasion of Cuba at the Bay of Pigs. The disaster was not solely military: it extended to every phase of American policy to create not merely a gap but a chasm of credibility. Hence the task of President Kennedy, still new in office, was to restore—even to create—confidence. To restore the prestige of the United States, both at home and abroad, President Kennedy needed all his talents, of which fortunately one was the ability to conceive lines of policy and to communicate them to others.

On June 23, 1961, six weeks after the fiasco at the Bay of Pigs, he met Nikita Khrushchev in Vienna. Apparently Khrushchev underestimated both the strength and the determination of the youthful president. Be that as it may, Khrushchev's threat to recognize East Germany, and thus to force the issue concerning the access of the allied powers to Berlin, required Kennedy to make a fateful decision. On July 25, 1961, he addressed the people of the United States in the most solemn tones. He told them that, if necessary, the United States would go to war to defend the freedom of Berlin. If war began, he said, it would begin in Moscow, where the Soviets had stirred up the crisis. He was prepared to triple the draft call and to summon reservists to active duty. The long-range nuclear bomber force was put on the alert. President Kennedy hoped that the actions he announced would persuade Khrushchev to change his policy. Nevertheless, he declared the United States would go to war, if necessary, rather than be driven out of Berlin.[1]

[1] This narrative of President Kennedy's visit to Berlin, and of his speech

The Kremlin gave way. The response was two-fold: a wall was erected to seal off the Communist sector of Berlin, and communications from Khrushchev to Kennedy indicated a Russian willingness for accommodation. The crisis over Berlin, followed by the Soviet breaking of the nuclear test ban, and the attempt in October, 1962, to install nuclear missiles in Cuba, left many considerations unknown to the Russians, to the Americans, and to the Berliners. But this much President Kennedy made unmistakingly clear:

It shall be the policy of this nation to regard any nuclear missile launched from Cuba against any nation in the Western Hemisphere as an attack by the Soviet Union on the United States, requiring a full retaliatory response on the Soviet Union.[2]

By June 26, 1963, two years after the June meeting with Khrushchev in Vienna, and a little more than two years after the Bay of Pigs disaster, Kennedy had generated confidence in his administration and apparently had convinced everyone, including the Kremlin, of his determination to defend the free peoples, including those of Berlin, where his prestige could hardly have been higher. On June 26 more than a million Berliners lined the streets to gain a glimpse of "Ken-ned-dee," and resounding shouts of "Ken-ned-dee" were heard along his way. The people of Berlin leaped and screamed along the curb as Kennedy's entourage passed by; they threw flowers and waved flags; some ran along his car in an endeavor to shake his hand—and some succeeded. Some threw bouquets—he caught two. One placard declared, "JOHN, YOU ARE OUR BEST FRIEND." Another caught the President's eye: *"ICH GRÜSSE CAROLINE."*[3] According to Pierre Salinger, the reception in Berlin was the greatest Kennedy had ever had.[4]

On this memorable day, the Communist regime of East Berlin hung red cloth from the pillars of the Brandenburg Gate, thus preventing the East Berliners from viewing the spectacle of Kennedy's reception, and preventing the Kennedy party from viewing East Berlin. Near the Brandenburg Gate, beyond the wall in East Berlin, the communists erected a placard:

---

in the Rudolphe Wilde Platz, is based on contemporary news dispatches and on the accounts in the books listed under "Further Reading."

2 Salinger, *With Kennedy,* p. 266.

3 *The New York Times,* Thursday, June 27, 1963.

4 *Ibid.*

In the agreements of Yalta and Potsdam U.S. Presidents Roosevelt
and Truman undertook:

To uproot German militarism and Naziism.

To arrest war criminals and bring them to judgment.

To prevent the rebirth of German militarism.

To ban all militarists and Nazi propaganda.

To ensure that Germany never again menaces her neighbors of
world peace.

Those pledges have been fulfilled in the German Democratic Republic. When will these pledges be fulfilled in West Germany and
Berlin, President Kennedy? [5]

Perhaps President Kennedy did not see the Communist
placard. In any event, it did not prevent the tumultuous welcome
accorded him in West Berlin, and it did not keep him from making five speeches, including one to an audience of at least 150,000
people. Nor did it keep President Kennedy from announcing to
the cheering throng in the Rudolphe Wilde Platz: *"Ich bin ein
Berliner."*

The Speech

ICH BIN EIN BERLINER

*I am proud to come to this city as the guest of your distin-
guished Mayor, who has symbolized throughout the world the
fighting spirit of West Berlin. And I am proud to visit the Federal Republic with your distinguished Chancellor who for so
many years has committed Germany to democracy and freedom
and progress, and to come here in the company of my fellow
American, General Clay, who has been in this city during its
great moments of crisis and will come again if ever needed.*

Two thousand years ago the proudest boast was "civis Romanus
sum." *Today, in the world of freedom, the proudest boast is "Ich
bin ein Berliner."*

I appreciate my interpreter translating my German!

*There are many people in the world who really don't under-
stand, or say they don't, what is the great issue between the free
world and the Communist world. Let them come to Berlin. There*

[5] *Ibid.*

are some who say that communism is the wave of the future. Let them come to Berlin. And there are some who say in Europe and elsewhere we can work with the Communists. Let them come to Berlin. And there are even a few who say that it is true that communism is an evil system, but it permits us to make economic progress. Lass' sie nach Berlin kommen. Let them come to Berlin.

Freedom has many difficulties and democracy is not perfect, but we have never had to put a wall up to keep our people in, to prevent them from leaving us. I want to say, on behalf of my countrymen, who live many miles away on the other side of the Atlantic, who are far distant from you, that they take the greatest pride that they have been able to share with you, even from a distance, the story of the last 18 years. I know of no town, no city, that has been besieged for 18 years that still lives with the vitality and the force, and the hope and the determination of the city of West Berlin. While the wall is the most obvious and vivid demonstration of the failures of the Communist system, for all the world to see, we take no satisfaction in it, for it is, as your Mayor has said, an offense not only against history but an offense against humanity, separating families, dividing husbands and wives and brothers and sisters, and dividing a people who wish to be joined together.

What is true of this city is true of Germany—real, lasting peace in Europe can never be assured as long as one German out of four is denied the elementary right of free men, and that is to make a free choice. In 18 years of peace and good faith, this generation of Germans has earned the right to be free, including the right to unite their families and their nation in lasting peace, with good will to all people. You live in a defended island of freedom, but your life is part of the main. So let me ask you, as I close, to lift your eyes beyond the dangers of today, to the hopes of tomorrow, beyond the freedom merely of this city of Berlin, or your country of Germany, to the advance of freedom everywhere, beyond the wall to the day of peace with justice, beyond yourselves and ourselves to all mankind.

Freedom is indivisible, and when one man is enslaved, all are not free. When all are free, then we can look forward to that day when this city will be joined as one and this country and this great Continent of Europe in a peaceful and hopeful globe. When

*that day finally comes, as it will, the people of West Berlin can
take sober satisfaction in the fact that they were in the front
lines for almost two decades.*

*All free men, wherever they may live, are citizens of Berlin,
and, therefore, as a free man, I take pride in the words* Ich bin
ein Berliner.

Further Reading

John F. Kennedy served his brief presidency during a fateful
period. Since his untimely death, a number of books emphasiz-
ing the events of his presidency have been published, and they
naturally provide information concerning his speechmaking. Theodore C. Sorenson's *Kennedy* (New York: Harper & Row, 1965)
offers (pp. 240–48) a fascinating account of the development of
Kennedy's "Inaugural Address." Other titles to be recommended
are Hugh F. Sidey, *John F. Kennedy: President* (New York:
Atheneum, 1963); Pierre Salinger, *With Kennedy* (Garden City,
New York: Doubleday & Co., Inc., 1966); Jim Bishop, *A Day in
the Life of President Kennedy* (New York: Random House,
1964); and Arthur Schlesinger, *A Thousand Days: John F. Kennedy in the White House* (Boston: Houghton Mifflin Co., 1965).

Three books by John F. Kennedy should be mentioned: *Why
England Slept* (New York: W. Funk, Inc., 1940); *A Nation of
Immigrants* (New York: Popular Library, 1964); and *Profiles in
Courage* (New York: Harper & Brothers, 1956). President Kennedy's views are also expressed in government documents and
official papers, as well as in the texts of his speeches, notably
those published in *The Strategy of Peace* (London: Hamish
Hamilton, 1960), in *To Turn the Tide* (New York: Harper &
Brothers, 1962), and in *The Great Debates: Background, Perspective, Effects* (Bloomington: Indiana University Press, 1962),
as edited by Sidney Kraus. President Kennedy's news conferences
are admirably reported in *Kennedy and the Press: The News
Conferences* (New York: Thomas Y. Crowell Co., 1965), as
edited and annotated by Harold W. Chase and Allen H. Lerman,
with an introduction by Pierre Salinger.

CHAPTER 20

Tribute to President Kennedy

THE RT. HON. HAROLD MACMILLAN

President Kennedy was a man of the highest physical and moral courage, tested and proved in war and in peace.

—THE RT. HON. HAROLD MACMILLAN

The Speaker

THE RT. HON. [MAURICE] HAROLD MACMILLAN was born in London on February 10, 1894, the son of Maurice Crawford and Helen (Belles) Macmillan. He served as Member of Parliament for Bromley from November, 1945, to September, 1964, and as Prime Minister and First Lord of the Treasury from January, 1957, to October, 1963. He was educated at Eton and at Balliol College, Oxford. During his service with the Special Reserve Grenadier Guards in World War I he was wounded three times. During World War II he was Parliamentary Secretary, Minister of Supply (1940–42) and Minister Resident at Allied Headquarters in Northwest Africa (1942–45).

Following World War II he held a number of offices in the British government: Minister of Housing and Local Government, Minister of Defense, Secretary of State for Foreign Affairs, and Chancellor of the Exchequer. In his parliamentary career he generally supported the policies of Sir Winston Churchill. He opposed the so-called "Peace of Munich." Following the rupture between the British and American governments over the Suez crisis, he sought diligently to improve relations and was considered successful in doing so.

In 1963 he assumed the chairmanship of Macmillan & Company, Ltd., the publishing firm of which his grandfather was one of the founders. On undergoing major surgery in October, 1963, he resigned as Prime Minister to be succeeded by Sir Alec Douglas-Home.

The text of the tribute to President Kennedy is taken from *Parliamentary Debates (Hansard) Fifth -Series—Volume 685 House of Commons Official Report, Fifth Session of the Forty-Second Parliament of the United Kingdom of Great Britain and Northern Ireland, Twelfth Year of the Reign of Her Majesty, Queen Elizabeth II: Session 1963–64 Comprising Period from 25th November—6th December, 1963* (London: H. M. Stationery Office), 40–42.

The Occasion

Following the death of President John F. Kennedy on November 22, 1963, the people of Britain, first in shocked disbelief and later in genuine sorrow, sought ways to express their compassion.[1] Americans in London were offered condolence as though a personal friend had died; indeed it seemed everywhere to be assumed that England and the world, as well as the United States, had lost a President. English people by the thousands trooped to the American Embassy in Grosvenor Square to sign a message of sympathy. Flags flew at half-mast. In an observance normally reserved for the death of royalty, cathedral bells were tolled. The Queen herself attended a special service in her chapel at Windsor Castle. As the Prime Minister and the official party

---

[1] The account of the responses of the people of Britain to the assassination of President Kennedy is drawn from the newspapers and from personal observations. The editors were living in Watford, about an hour by the underground from Westminster, in November, 1963. The statements concerning Mr. Macmillan's speech are based on observations made during the speech, which was witnessed by one of the editors, who was seated in the Commonwealth section of the galleries.

left London for Washington and the funeral of the President, the other national leaders remained to attend a commemoration in Westminster Cathedral, an event notable also because for the first time in the knowledge of learned men both Catholic and Protestant clergymen participated in a common ceremony. One had the feeling that something more than formal courtesy impelled the manifestations, both personal and official, to be observed everywhere. Perhaps a renewal of the comradeship that seemed to exist during World War II could explain in part the concern expressed. Perhaps only the tie of a common language, of blood thicker than water, of bonds of kinship remembered in time of stress, could account for the sense of shared affliction.

The spirit prevailing in the homes and on the streets extended to the House of Commons. When the House convened at Westminster on Monday, November 25, following the death of President Kennedy, the session was given over to tributes to the late President. From the Chair Mr. Speaker stated his assumption that the House would wish him to proceed, in contravention of its rules, to entertain a motion on which the required notice had not been given, whereupon R. A. Butler, Secretary of State for Foreign Affairs, presented the following manuscript motion:

That an humble Address be presented to Her Majesty praying Her Majesty to be graciously pleased to express to the President of the United States of America the shock and deep sorrow with which this House has learned of the death of President Kennedy; and to convey their sense of the loss which this country and the Commonwealth have sustained, and their profound sympathy with Mrs. Kennedy and the family of the late President, and with the Government and people of the United States of America.[2]

Mr. Butler spoke to the motion, and was followed by Gordon Walker and Donald Wade, who spoke appropriately for their constituents. The Rt. Hon. Harold Macmillan, until recently Prime Minister, and still member of Parliament for Bromley, then rose to address the House of Commons. As he spoke quietly, it seemed almost dispassionately, the House gave complete attention. The House of Commons is sometimes a noisy, even an unruly, body that Mr. Speaker must call to order. On this occasion, however, the members observed full decorum. Doubtless

[2] *Parliamentary Debates, op. cit.*

the members were impressed, as were some persons in the galleries, that Mr. Macmillan should appear in the House; for it was well-known that he had recently undergone major surgery. On this appearance, his first since hospitalization, Mr. Macmillan's pallor, and his somewhat subdued manner, reminded his hearers of his own mortality and testified to his faithfulness in rising from a sick bed to speak words of affection and respect for John F. Kennedy. Adorned only with the prestige of his personal commitment to the language he employed and with his high ethical proof, Mr. Macmillan's speech was truly moving in the modern eloquence that persuades without shouts, without display, without excess of vigor, but with the conviction of power latent in the language and the character of the speaker.

The Speech

TRIBUTE TO PRESIDENT KENNEDY

With the permission of the House I would like to add a few words to the eloquent tributes to the memory of President Kennedy which have been paid on behalf of all the three great parties in our country.

My right hon. Friend the Foreign Secretary and the right hon. Member for Smethwick (Mr. Gordon Walker) and the hon. Member for Huddersfield, West (Mr. Wade), who followed, have expressed in moving phrases the sympathy which we in the House, aye, and the whole people of Britain, feel with the people of the United States at this tragic moment in their history.

They have also made it abundantly clear that we here, and throughout the Commonwealth, share their sorrow to the full, for we do not merely mourn a grievous loss to the vigour and vitality of American public life; we mourn a world statesman, to whose leadership, in these critical but inspiring days, all the peoples of the world, of whatever race, creed or colour, looked with confidence and hope.

My only purpose in rising is to add a few sentences as a friend and, in a true sense, a colleague. For three years he and I worked in the closest association. Every few months we met—sometimes on British and sometimes on American soil—and in between we interchanged frequent messages and telephone talks. Anyone who knew the President could not fail to realise that behind the captivating charm of manner lay an immense fund of deeply pondered knowledge on a wide range of subjects—political, economic, military. He was one of the best-informed statesmen whom it has ever been my lot to meet, but he was altogether without pedantry or any trace of intellectual arrogance.

The President was very fond of asking questions and trying to find out other people's views. He was chary of giving his own opinion except after much reflection and consideration. Admirably briefed as he always was by his staff, he never stuck slavishly to a brief. Unlike some men with whom discussion is often almost a formality, he was always ready to listen to and to be convinced by argument. In this way he brought to the baffling problems of today a remarkable freshness of mind and flexibility of approach. These were based upon his fundamental moral and mental integrity.

President Kennedy was a man of the highest physical and moral courage, tested and proved in war and in peace.

When things were difficult, almost desperate, he was both resourceful and resolute. When things seemed a bit easier, he displayed a boyish and infectious delight which was irresistible. Although his career has been cut short so tragically, he will stand high even among the great names of great American Presidents.

In this country we shall always remember him as a sincere and loyal friend of Britain. To the whole world without distinction his life and words and actions were a constant inspiration. He did not regard it as a statesman's duty to yield to public opinion, but to strive to lead it. Subjected to great pressures on many conflicting issues, he seemed sometimes to be almost a rather lonely figure, but always true to his own integrity and his own faith. What he said, he meant, and he did his best to accomplish. To him the words "peace and progress" were not just a phrase for a peroration, but a living and burning faith.

So it was, as has been said already, that when that terrible news came on Friday everyone in this country—and, I think, in every country—felt stunned by the shock of what seemed to us —to each one of us—a personal bereavement, and to the whole of humanity, struggling in this world of darkness, the sudden and cruel extinction of a shining light.

*We mourn for him and for his bereaved family, to whom we
offer our respectful sympathy, and for all the American people;
and we mourn him—and this is perhaps the greatest tribute to
Jack Kennedy's life and work—for ourselves, for what we and all
the world have lost.*

Further Reading

For the texts of Mr. Macmillan's speeches one must resort for
the most part to the *Parliamentary Debates*. News accounts and
reviews contemporary with his career afford another, if sometimes prejudiced, source of information. A book by Emrys
Hughes, *Macmillan: Portrait of a Politician* (London: George
Allen & Unwin, Ltd., 1962), published while Macmillan was still
Prime Minister, is useful chiefly for excerpts from the British
press and from the documents. Harold Macmillan's own book,
Winds of Change: 1914–1939 (New York: Harper & Row, 1966),
is interesting reading and a good account of Macmillan's life during the period it covers. Additional volumes covering the years
since 1939 are now in progress.